Stock Investing
Stock Market Investing For Beginners

Simple Stock Investing Guide To Become An Intelligent Investor And Make Money In Stocks

© **Copyright 2017 by David Morales - All rights reserved.**

This document is geared towards providing exact and reliable information in regards to the topic and issue covered. The publication is sold with the idea that the publisher is not required to render accounting, officially permitted, or otherwise, qualified services. If advice is necessary, legal or professional, a practiced individual in the profession should be ordered.

- From a Declaration of Principles which was accepted and approved equally by a Committee of the American Bar Association and a Committee of Publishers and Associations.

In no way is it legal to reproduce, duplicate, or transmit any part of this document in either electronic means or in printed format. Recording of this publication is strictly prohibited and any storage of this document is not allowed unless with written permission from the publisher. All rights reserved.

The information provided herein is stated to be truthful and consistent, in that any liability, in terms of inattention or otherwise, by any usage or abuse of any policies, processes, or directions contained within is the solitary and utter responsibility of the recipient reader. Under no circumstances will any legal responsibility or blame be held against the publisher for any reparation, damages, or monetary loss due to the information herein, either directly or indirectly.

Respective authors own all copyrights not held by the publisher.

The trademarks that are used are without any consent, and the publication of the trademark is without permission or backing by the trademark owner. All trademarks and brands within this book are for clarifying purposes only and are the owned by the owners themselves, not affiliated with this document.

Table of Contents

Chapter 1: Stop! Read This Before You Start 7

Chapter 2: Remember- There are No Guarantees with Stock Investing..14

Chapter 3: Create a Timeline for Systematic Investing.........22

Chapter 4: Stock Trading Terms and Operations in Basic English (Part 1) 25

Chapter 5 : Stock Trading Terms in Basic English (Part 2)..34

Chapter 6: Know the Importance of Trading Strategies 39

Chapter 7: Swing Trading..49

Chapter 8: Day Trading 57

Chapter 9: Position Trading 61

Chapter 10: Value Investing..68

Chapter 11: Playing the Stock Market through Mutual Funds 77

Chapter 12: Make Sure you have the Right Tools to Trade Profitably...81

Chapter 13: Day Trading Tactics...84

Chapter 14: Position Trading Tactics...93

Chapter 15: Value Trading Tactics 98

Conclusion 102

Introduction

This is my personal stock trading story: I started trading stocks when I got my first part time job while I was still in college. You might think that this was a pretty great start. After all, most people never really start stock investing until they are already established in their careers. In fact, the average American trades stock primarily as a passive investor as part of that person's 401k plan at work. Put simply, most people don't actively look to invest in stocks.

You might think that I had a great early start with investing. Well, not quite. While Microsoft, Apple, Cisco and other amazing companies were trading at the time I started investing in stocks, I didn't invest in those stocks. If I did, I'd be worth hundreds of millions of dollars today. In fact, when I started investing, Cisco, Apple and Microsoft were trading at very low prices.

What I did was I just dove into stock investing and bought whatever "cheap" companies were being recommended by investment "experts" featured in the newspapers I read at that time. I only paid attention to two factors: the price of the stock and where it was in its 52 week valuation. If the stock was trading near its 52 week low, and the stock was affordable as far as my budget was concerned, I bought the stock.

I did not look into its industry, I did not do research regarding the company's market position. In many cases, I didn't even know if the company was making any money. I only looked at whether it was recommended by experts and whether it was cheap enough. Every pay check I would set aside a few hundred dollars to buy these "cheap" stocks I was told had a "tremendous upside."

As I mentioned, I didn't bother to do thorough industry research, nor did I pay attention to the stock's momentum, volume and other crucial trading details. The result? Of the 5 companies I invested in, 2 went bankrupt. One is still around, but it's a dormant "shell" company that is a penny stock. To make matters worse, it barely trades. The other two companies that I bought, I ended up selling them for prices that were lower than I bought them for.

Fast Forward to Today

Now, I make money on all my trades. I know when to buy in, and I know when to sell. In fact, it has become quite predictable to me. While I don't always rack up daily profits in the 5 digit range, I definitely have come a very long way from when I began trading. I actually make a profit every single day.

I've got some great news for you: if I can go from a hype-crazed foolish investor throwing good money after bad on lousy stocks to someone who can reliably pick winning stocks, so can you. The only difference between you and me is information.

This book spells out the information you need to begin your stock trading career the right way. Don't begin it the same way I did. I lost money. I worked hard for that money while I was going to college and all that money just went up in smoke. Learn from my mistakes.

Indeed, this book is a compilation of the hard lessons I've learned trading stocks through the years. Put simply, I focused on the things that work. I focused on the information you need to pay attention to so you can become a successful stock trader.

There are Tons of Investment Books Out There

Let's just get one thing out of the way, while it's true that this book is yet another of many stock investment books in the marketplace, most of those stock investment books have it all wrong. This book is intended to help newbie traders such as you to cut through the hype and fluff and get to the good stuff as quickly as possible.

You need to avoid my mistakes and benefit from what I got right. By getting the right information from the very beginning, you put yourself in a better position. You increase your chances of trading profitably, consistently. I can't emphasize the word "consistently" enough.

Make no mistake about it, anybody can get lucky from time to time. Unfortunately, luck is not going to put food on the table. Luck can fall short. You need a clear idea as to what works so you can trade with a higher chance of consistent profit.

Stock Trading is a Journey

I wish I could tell you that, just by reading this book, you will become a millionaire. Unfortunately, nobody can make that guarantee. You have to understand that stock trading is a journey. Just like any trip, it involves growth. It involves changing your perspective and, yes, it involves overcoming challenges.

This book steps you through the jungle of confusing "stock market talk" and terms and puzzling "strategies." Instead, I explain strategies in clear, everyday English, so you can make truly informed decisions when looking for trading opportunities, timing your buying and selling, and reinvesting your profits.

I wish you the very best in your journey into the amazing and richly rewarding world of stock trading!

Chapter 1: Stop! Read This Before You Start

Before you get all excited about diving into this book and putting it into action, I need to stop you in your tracks. You can't just jump in with both feet and start opening online brokerage accounts and trading away. It doesn't work that way. You have to make sure that you have the preliminary steps out of the way. Otherwise, you're simply doing things randomly and you're doing things based on emotion.

While I appreciate the fact that you are excited about this whole venture, it's too easy to trade impulsively. It's too easy to make investment decisions that aren't based on facts. It's crucial that you make sure that you have the basics out of the way so you can increase your chances of being successful in stock trading.

Please pay attention to the following questions. They will help you get prepared properly for your journey into stock trading.

Do You Have the Time to Research?

Make no mistake about it, when it comes to stock trading, you have to research and you have to do it right. This takes time. Most people think they know how to research, but it turns out that they have no clue. You have to give yourself the time and the space to do adequate research on the stocks that you will be buying or research on stock trading strategies.

There are certain strategies that don't require you to research the stock. You only need to pay attention to the volume and trader activity in that stock. The key question here is whether you have the time to do proper research on whatever trading strategy you're going to be pursuing so you can increase your chances of being successful.

Are You Curious Enough?

A lot of people read books because they're desperate for information. They just look at books to solve a problem. Now, there's nothing wrong with that, but if you really want to take things to a much higher level as far as your trading success goes, you have to be curious.

You can't just look for information, you also have to pay attention to the implications. You also have to be curious as to how to connect the dots and whether knowing one piece of information can lead to another piece of information. That's how you can learn powerful strategies in no time at all. It all depends on your curiosity.

For people who aren't curious, all of this can be a chore. It can be a hassle for them. Their hearts are not in it and they're only doing it because they need to make money quickly. I hope you can see the difference. If you're curious, you are more likely to come up with interesting solutions as well as spot potential problems. This leads to you being able to identify greater opportunities.

Do You Have Funds Ready to Invest?

This part is really important. If you want to trade in stock, you need to make sure that you have proper capital. Do you have money to invest now? If not, when will you be ready?

Don't Expect to Hit a Homerun the First Time You Step Up to the Plate and Swing the Bat!

This should be quite obvious. I'm sure the first time you played basketball, you didn't expect that you're going to play like Michael Jordan on the court. Most people don't have that expectation.

However, you'd be surprised as to how many people think that just because they're trading in stocks that their investments are going to be all winners. It doesn't work that way. In many cases, your expectations can end up sabotaging you. So do yourself a big favor and make sure that your expectations are realistic.

What is the most realistic expectation you should have? Expect to learn. That is always my mindset and it has never let me down. You need to set the right expectations, otherwise, you might become so discouraged by your results that you end up quitting. I'm sure you already know that the only way you can fail is to quit. That's the only way you can lose.

Be Clear About Your Initial Goals

It's really important at this stage to also be clear as to why you're investing. This is really important. What are your goals? What are you going to do with the money that you will make?

This, of course, turns on how old you are. If you are somebody who is 50 years old and is a decade or slightly more away from retirement, your investment goals are going to be vastly different than if you were 22 years old and fresh out of college, or a 19 year old and you just graduated high school.

Age matters when setting up investment goals because you can afford to take a lot more risks when you are younger. How come? Well, if you were like me and you invested in really speculative stocks when you were 19, even if all your stocks tanked, you still have a lot of time for you to get the capital together and try again.

This is not the case if you are 50 years old and you're looking at 15 more years until you retire. In that particular situation, it pays to be a little bit more conservative. Do you see the difference? It can take quite a while for you to raise the money again from your work or other sources of income.

Keep this is mind, your age has a big impact on what your investment goals and investment styles should be.

Investing for Retirement Vs. Investing for Growth

If you're investing for retirement, you're basically just looking for a reliable growth rate. This is not super sexy, you're not going to be greeted by eye popping returns that blow away the market average. Instead, you just want a steady return that beats inflation. Put simply, you have money now that you have saved through all those years of working and you want to make sure that your money retains its value long after you've retired. This is why investing for retirement is focused primarily on conservative investments like utility stocks and blue chip stocks.

On the other hand, if you are younger, you can invest for growth. This investment goal involves investing in companies that are very speculative or maybe unpredictable. Your main focus is to grow your money as quickly as possible while, of course, accepting the risks that go with such amazing growth.

These two scenarios spell out the different investment goals people have. But if this is your first time investing, your initial goal should be to simply learn. That's right. When you open that brokerage account and you start trading, tell yourself that the way you're going to measure profits or loss is based on how much you learned. This way, you don't get terribly disappointed if your trades don't pan out. Again, it's all about expectations.

Why do you Need to Invest?

Let me cut straight to the chase. Regardless of whether you're a conservative investor that is soon going to go into retirement or you're a young person just out of high school or college, you need to know why you need to invest. This is really important because a lot of people think that stock investing is just another option out there besides saving.

Well, they are two totally different things. A lot of people are under the mistaken assumption that as long as they save money from their income and set aside a certain percentage religiously, month after month, year after year, decade after decade, they will be fine. I'm sorry to disappoint you, but that is not a winning strategy.

In fact, you are playing the game to lose if you are just going to rely on your savings. Why? There is this thing called inflation. Put in the simplest terms possible, inflation is an economic effect where the amount of goods and services one dollar buys this year is going to be worth less next year and the year after that, and so on and so forth. Ultimately, you reach a point where your dollar is no longer able to buy much of anything.

If you think this is crazy or far fetched, you only need to realize that back in the 1800's, a full time salary for somebody was a few dollars per month. Obviously, people can't live on that now. That just goes to show you the power of inflation because a dollar back in 1860 is worth so much more now in terms of today's dollar's purchasing power. That's how bad inflation can be.

Even if you looked at as recently as 10 years ago, the food that you could have bought back then, you can no longer buy now. For example, if you walk into a Taco Bell and spend money on a burrito, that money that you spent 10 years ago, is probably not going to buy the same amount of burritos today.

Inflation is a serious problem and simply saving money is not going to fix it. You have to find a way to grow your money. This is why stocks are so hot. Stock investing enables you to beat inflation.

If inflation is going up at a rate of 2-5% a year, you can rest on the fact that, if you put your money in a general stock fund that tracks the market index, your money may grow 10-15% per year. In other words, you beat inflation by as much as 13% or as little as 5%. Whatever the case may be, you're still beating inflation. Your money is not losing its value.

Historically speaking, stocks have appreciated in the range of between 12% to over 15% per year. That is amazing inflation protection. While real estate can give you better returns on average, real estate also can suffer a reversal.

If you don't believe me, look at the average real estate values in the United States as a whole after the great financial crash of 2008. You'd be surprised as to how quickly million dollar homes went down in value. While real estate, generally speaking, offers a great amount of inflation protection, you would be better off with stock investing.

Advantages of Stocks over Real Estate

Without going into too much detail, it's a much better idea to invest in stocks than real estate. While both do provide you with a large measure of inflation protection, stocks are more fluid. You can simply go online to your online brokerage and place an order to sell your stock position and you're done with it. You've cashed out of your position.

This is not the case with real estate. You have to hire a broker or agent and wait possibly months or even years to unload your property. Real estate is simply not that liquid. Also, real estate's appreciation depends primarily on location.

With stocks, you can buy a whole basket of stocks through a mutual fund and if the mutual fund management company is any good, you can at least track the performance of the general market. This is not the case with real estate. You might end up in a local real estate market that under-performs the national average quite a bit.

Also, in terms of the money that you need to put together to invest, it takes quite a bit of money to invest in real estate. You have to at least put up the down payment required by the bank to give you a loan for the rest of the asking price of the property that you're buying.

With stocks, you have a lot more leeway. You know, coming in, how much you will be paying. Maybe you have a tight budget, so you might want to look for stocks that are trading at fairly low prices, but have a high momentum or a high growth potential.

You have a lot more freedom as far as investing in stocks is concerned. If you don't have the time to research, you can take a fairly small amount of cash and invest it in a mutual fund.

In the next chapter, I'm going to cover the concept of risk. Stay tuned because this is extremely important in helping you plan out your stock investment strategy.

Chapter 2: Remember- There are No Guarantees with Stock Investing

Unlike real estate investing, there are basically no guarantees with stock investing. While it's true that there also no guarantees with real estate, you can actually minimize your losses. In fact, you can avoid losses altogether by simply just hanging onto your property.

For example, you bought a commercial property that is worth $3 million at the time of purchase. The local real estate market collapses and for the next 5 years, the value of your property is $1 million. Now, you can choose to sell at a loss. If you're desperate for the cash or you're having a tough time keeping up with payments to the bank, you can liquidate your position and sell at a loss.

Alternatively, you can hang on to your property until the local market recovers. This actually happens quite a bit, where people simply hang on to their property and end up selling for double the price they paid. You just have to weather the storm. Depending on your financial position, this can help you achieve a great return in the future.

This is not the case with stocks. A stock can crash to zero. Seriously. In the story that I told you in the introduction of this book, I bought a company that does missile testing for the US Department of Defense. It was a hot stock back during the Cold War, but, as you can well imagine, after the Soviet Union collapsed, defense companies started going belly up. The stock that I bought for quite a bit of money back then, is now a penny stock that barely trades.

The lesson here is that you can lose money with stock investing. There is no guarantee that your investment will hold its value. I need to make this clear because you need to have a realistic understanding of the concept of risk.

Most People Have Risk All Wrong

Usually, when people come across the word "risk," they always think of negative things. They think about what they're risking, meaning, what they stand to lose. They think about all the things that could go wrong. They think about retiring with very little money. They think about all sorts of negative scenarios and it all revolves around the concept of loss. How likely is it that you will lose money? That's how most people define risk.

What if I told you that this is the wrong definition? From an investor or trader's perspective, risk actually has a different definition. Risk is an indicator of how much reward a potential investment brings to the table. As the old saying goes, the higher the risk, the higher the reward.

Well, professional traders look for certain levels of risk because they are looking for rewards that they cannot get with conventional stock investments. If you talk to a hedge fund manager, they would tell you that they consciously look for investments that have a certain risk profile that is normally higher than the risk associated with certain types of stocks.

There are certain stocks that are not very risky. These stocks pay a dividend. These stocks also have a fixed base of customers. They're not going to go away anytime soon. I am, of course, talking about stocks like utilities.

But there are other stocks that fit that profile. While they do move in price, they tend to move within a fixed range. The problem with those stocks is, if you are looking for a nice, big return, you probably won't get it playing those stocks. That's why experienced hedge fund managers, as well as even mutual fund managers, are looking for riskier stocks.

I need you to understand how risk works. It's not necessarily something that you have to run away from. It's not something that should turn you off or scare you. Instead, it's an indicator of what the potential upside is. Of course, it's also an indicator of how likely it is that you would lose your money.

You have to be clear early on what your risk profile is. Ask yourself the following questions: How much risk can you take? How much risk do you want to take? Are you the type of person who worries a lot? Are you the type of person who is a big believer in taking risks because you believe that to get big rewards, you need to take big risks? Are you a risk averse person?

Again, as I've mentioned in the previous chapter, your age must play a big role in your risk profile. Personality wise, you might be a daredevil. You might be all about risk taking. That's all well and good, but if you are in your 60's, you might want to slow down. You might want to be at least a little bit more conservative as far as your financial investments are concerned.

Always factor in your age because, again, you have to remember that if you fail and lose your money, you need time to get that money back. Obviously, if you're younger, you have a higher chance of doing this. If you're older, your options are much more limited.

Stock Investing Vs. Bond Investing

Stock investing involves buying ownership shares in a publicly traded company. You are, for the record, an owner of that company. Don't get too excited. The total number of shares the company issues might be in the tens of millions. So if you own two shares of a company, your ownership stake is in the millionth. Still, you are, legally speaking, a part owner of that company.

The great thing about being a stockholder is that you have ownership rights, but your legal liability is limited. If the company does something wrong and they get sued, the people who succeed in the lawsuit cannot come after you and your personal assets. They can just take the assets of the company and the only thing that you would lose is, of course, the stock value of the company when it takes a hit in the market or goes bankrupt. Still, your losses are limited.

With stock investing, you make money on the appreciation of the value of the stock. If you are doing short sales or short selling, you make money when the stock crashes and you buy it back at a much lower price. Whatever the case may be, you are making money off the fluctuations in the market price of the stock of the company you are an owner of.

Bond investing, on the other hand, is completely different. You're not an owner. Instead, you are a creditor to the company. The company needs money, so they issue an IOU to the general public. This IOU has an interest rate that the company will pay.

If you buy bonds, you are basically buying the right to collect that interest. Now, there is a secondary market for bonds, and this is why there is such a thing as bond yields. You can buy and sell bonds based on market demand.

Usually, yields and bond prices go in opposite directions. If a company is in trouble, its bond yield goes up because people are ditching the bond. If people are flocking to buy the bond, the opposite effect takes place. The bonds yield crashes. It means that there is a tremendous amount of buying interest in the bond. Whatever the case may be, keep in mind that with bond investing, you are making money either through the yield of the bond, or through the interest that you collect by holding the bond.

A lot of traders buy and sell bonds like stock, but the fundamental difference here is a bond is essentially a loan to you. If the company, for any reason, goes belly up, bond holders are near the front of the line as far as getting portions of the remaining assets of the company that went bankrupt.

Before You Trade, Select a Strategy Based on Your Risk Appetite

Now that you've asked yourself the key questions outlined above, you need to select a strategy that fits your risk appetite. Keep in mind that there's a big difference between your risk profile and your risk appetite.

I've already covered your risk profile. It really boils down to your age. If you are not in a position to quickly recover from a bad investment decision, then you have a very low risk profile. Now, if you are fairly young and aggressive, you have a high risk profile.

Risk profile determines the kinds of investments you should entertain because different investments carry different risk levels. If you have a fairly low risk profile, then you should look for low risk investments like utilities. On the other hand, if you have a fairly high risk profile, then you might want to consider text stocks like Facebook.

Risk profile is different from risk appetite. Risk appetite has more to do with your personality. What kind of investor are you? Are you the type of person that is just looking for a sure return or something close to it? Or you the type of person who is looking for very big returns, knowing full well that you can lose your money overnight? You are looking for very big returns in a relatively short period of time. You are able to sleep at night knowing full well that when you wake up tomorrow, most of your money might be gone.

So how does this all Impact your Investment Strategy?

Well, if you have a low risk appetite, the best strategy for you would be value investing. This is the investment strategy used by the world famous multi-billionaire investor, Warren Buffet.

Mr. Buffet is easily one of the most powerful and successful investors in history. He started out with very little and, now, his holdings are just phenomenal. He's always in the top ten lists of the world's richest people.

He looks for value in companies that the market might be overlooking. Also, he looks for value not just in terms of the company doing well next year or the year after that, but five, ten or even twenty years down the road. And when he buys into a company, he buys big. In fact, in some cases, he actually completely took over the company because he believed in it so much.

On the other end of the spectrum are extremely risky investing strategies. One of these is day trading. With day trading, you're not really paying attention to the fundamental value of a stock. You're not paying attention to whether the stock is poised to become a market leader in three years or five years. You really don't care about any of that. All you care about is whether there is movement in the stock today that might indicate that it can go up in value. Put simply, your job is to buy a stock low for today, and then by the end of the day, sell it at a high enough level that you make money.

What makes this really risky is day traders borrow money for their stock purchases. For example, if you only had $10,000 in your own name and you're trading a stock that you bought at $10 and sold at $11 at the end of the day, if you were to rely only on your own money, you made a thousand dollars. But a day trader would borrow money from the brokerage he or she uses to increase the value of their starting capital.

Depending on your broker platform, you can borrow up to four times the amount of money you actually have. Using our example, instead of settling for $1,000 a day, you can get a margin account that inflates your money by a factor of 4 to 1. So in this scenario, your purchasing power is $40,000, so your profit is $4,000. Not too bad.

You then pay interest off your profit. The interest, if you pay your margin account quickly, is not that big in relation to the game you enjoyed. How much money would you rather make? $1,000 or $4,000 per day? I thought so.

How Much Time are You Giving Yourself?

In determining your risk profile, you need to also ask yourself how much time are you giving yourself to make money trading stocks. Do you give yourself a day? Can you afford a week? Are you okay with a month?

Now, this is a very important question to ask because it depends on how badly you need the money. Day traders are perfectly happy with making a couple of thousand dollars a day because they need to make that money every single day. Others have a longer time horizon because they are perfectly okay with their stock appreciating by 20% over a year.

Others like Warren Buffet, are perfectly okay with fairly slow rates of appreciation in the immediate term, as long as the overall long term prospects of the company are very bright indeed. Do you see the difference between these scenarios? You have to be clear as to which type of investor you are.

Would you rather Trade Directly or Through a Professional Manager?

Finally, now that you are interested in investing in stocks, ask yourself whether you'd rather trade personally or use the services of a professional fund manager. The great thing about using mutual funds is that they are managed by people who know how the stock market works and have some sort of track record.

Now, this is not a guarantee that they will make you money, but they've been around the block. They know how the game works and, if anything, they can at least get you close to the average return the market produces.

If you choose to trade directly on a personal basis, your returns might be much better or it might be much worse because you're still learning. You have to make this decision because this is a very important decision. It impacts how much you're going to make off your investments while you're still learning.

Chapter 3: Create a Timeline for Systematic Investing

It's really important for you to have a timeline in which you factor in your learning curve. You have to understand that, when it comes to anything in life, there are always two ways to do things. You can do things the easy way, and you can do things the hard way.

Usually, the easy way is also the smarter way of doing things. Unfortunately, most people would rather tackle things by the seat of their pants. They just dive in and they think that stock investing, just like with most other things in their lives, is something to learn as you go along. While there is a lot of truth to that, it can be a very expensive learning experience if you're not systematic.

This is why it's really important to pace yourself as you learn to invest. Don't try to rush into it; don't try to just digest as much as you can master the game overnight. I'm telling you, it's not going to happen. The worst part is you would end up burning through a lot of cash for you to learn that lesson. There are cheaper ways to learn that lesson and pacing plays a big role in minimizing your costs.

You have to remember that learning how to invest actually costs you both time and money. You're investing your time and you're also investing money. If you think about it hard enough, your more precious asset is not your money. Money can always be earned. It can definitely be borrowed. Time, on the other hand, is extremely fragile.

Once you spend time on anything, you can't get that time back. The best part about time is that it can turn into anything that you want. For example, if you invest time in working out at the gym, what do you think will happen after a few weeks or a few months? That's right. Not only can you lose weight, but you might actually also look much better. You'd be more muscular, you'd be more toned, and you might become healthier overall.

Similarly, if you invest time in your mind by reading a lot of books, you can become a very knowledgeable person, especially if you focus on reading very specialized books, like stock investing. You can become an expert. That's how important and precious time is.

It's too easy for people to waste their time by simply refusing to be systematic in their efforts at learning how to invest. You have to adopt some sort of timeline so you can properly pace yourself. There are a lot of things to cover. There are a lot of things to wrap your mind around. It's not just a simple matter of going through a list of options, picking one, and getting lucky. How I wish that were the case.

Successful stock investing doesn't work that way. If you want to constantly make great decisions, you can't hope to get lucky.

The Importance of Going through a Process

Now that I have made it clear to you that you have to have some sort of timeline, the next step is to realize that you need to go through a process. There are several phases in learning how to invest properly. You need to go through the proper stages and make sure you do a good job. You can't just rush through everything. I know you're busy, all of us are, but if you want to increase the likelihood that you will actually make money trading stocks, then you need to not only pace yourself properly, but go through the right phases.

There are 4 phases to learning stock investing. First, you're going to go through the education phase. Next, you're going to take action.

Whatever you've learned in the education phase, you're going to actually implement.

Next, you're going to fine tune what you're doing. Spoiler alert, the first few times you try to trade, chances are, you're not going to do all that well. Maybe your money remains the same and the stock tracks sideways. More likely, you end up losing a little bit of money. Regardless, you need to fine tune your trading so you can achieve better outcomes in the future.

Finally, the final stage is refined action. You refine the actions that you take to increase the likelihood that you would make better stock trades. This puts you on the road to constantly making money off stocks.

Remember, anybody can get lucky with a few stock trades here and there and make some money off the stock market, but it takes a systematic approach that is process driven for you to consistently make money. Now, this is not a guarantee that you're constantly going to make money, but you would be in a better position if you adopt this process. We're going to go through all 4 phases in this book.

Chapter 4: Stock Trading Terms and Operations in Basic English (Part 1)

Whenever you read any kind of stock investment guide or book, it's too easy to just get beaten up by all the jargon. It's too easy to get clobbered by all the technical terms. I'm going to spare you of all of that by speaking in plain English.

I'll try to strip down these terms into their simplest forms so not only can you understand them more quickly, but you would be able to relate these concepts to each other. This increases the likelihood that you would not be intimidated by stock trading.

This is one common problem that I see over and over again. A lot of people who'd like to go into stock trading and investing get intimidated because they think that it's all technical, that they're in way over their head. In fact, they get so scared that they feel that they're just basically going to lose money, hand over fist.

That doesn't have to be the case, and stripping down the terms into easy to understand forms can go a long way in making you less intimated. The less intimidated you are, the more your curiosity can take over and you can learn what you need to learn to do a good job in trading with a constant level of success.

Return on Investment (ROI)

Return on investment is a measurement of how much money you actually made on your investment. You look at how much money you ended up with after you placed your investment and deducting the costs for that investment. To illustrate, if stock in a company costs

$5,000 to buy, and you sold at $7,000, your total return on investment is $2,000 expressed in terms of a percentage. For example, you invested $5,000 and the total that you got back after one year in the stock market is $7,000, your actual profit is $2,000, which represents a percentage gain of 40%. This is your return on investment.

Now, keep in mind that you have to factor in time for determining return on investment. If it took you two years to get that $2,000 dollar gain, then your return on investment is 20% on a year-to-year basis. Always factor in the time spent invested in a particular stock position when determining return on investment.

Stocks

Stocks are shares of ownership in a company. These stocks are publicly traded. People from all over the world, for the most part, can buy stocks in any American company.

These stocks are sold at first in the form of an initial public offering. This is called the primary market. When a company sells stock for the first time, it trades in the primary market.

Once the stock is already public, and the shares are then purchased or kept by brokers, whatever trading that follows is secondary trading. In other words, the stock is selling in the secondary market. People are just buying and selling the rights to ownership of particular companies.

How Stocks get traded

Stocks get traded primarily through exchanges. Now, you might be thinking that a stock exchange involves a lot of people yelling at each other, buying and selling stocks. Well, this is how it used to be done. Back in the old days, brokers would actually have representatives on a trading floor, and they would buy and sell orders back and forth. In fact, these traders would even come up with fancy hand signals to communicate quickly how much stock they are buying and selling.

Fast-forward to today. Presently, all stocks are traded electronically. In a blink of an eye, millions of shares of stocks can get bought and sold. In fact, there are many trading platforms that take advantage of very fast trade executions to make fractional profits. Now, you may be thinking that half a penny is not that big of a deal. Well, it actually translates to a pretty decent chunk of money if we are talking about buy-and-sell orders that are worth tens of millions of dollars.

Stock Brokerages

Stock brokerages are firms that specialize in buying and selling stocks for their clients. Stock brokerages also hold stocks. These are called market makers. These stocks are owned by the brokerage houses, and they can be traded by speculators.

For example, somebody is going to sell a stock short, hoping that a stock will crash in price so that person can then buy that stock back at a cheaper price and pocket the difference. That person would have to "borrow" that stock from a stock brokerage. Brokerages are in the business of holding stocks and facilitating trades.

Trading Fees

When you work with a stock brokerage, you are giving them instructions to buy and sell stocks for you. You pay a fee for those services. Usually, the bigger your order, the smaller, in terms of percentage, the fees get. Nowadays, due to electronic trading, a lot of stock brokerages actually charge a flat rate. You can trade a huge amount of stock for a relatively small fee. These brokerages make money through volume.

Buying Long

What does it mean when somebody buys a stock "long?" When you are buying long, you are buying at a price that you think is low with the expectation that this price will get higher over time. Your strategy is very simple. You are buying low and then selling high. You are in it for "the long haul."

Well, it turns out that buying long does not necessarily mean long stretches of time. You can have a fixed time frame for you to sell, or you can even set a percentage gain that triggers your account to sell. Instead of buying and keeping stock for a lengthy period of time, buying long simply means that you are expecting that stock to appreciate in value and subsequently sell at that higher price to lock in your profits.

Selling Short

When you sell a stock short, what you actually end up doing is you are selling stock at a high price and thereafter buying it back once it crashes. The difference, of course, is your profit. Now, you may be thinking this seems impossible since where do you get the stock if you do not own it? How can you sell something that you do not own? Good question.

When you sell short, you are basically working with a brokerage that your brokerage networks with to borrow the stock that you are selling. At a certain point in time, you are going to have to "cover" that short position. In other words, you have to buy the underlying stock at that lower price. Selling short can be a very lucrative trading strategy if you have a high degree of confidence that a stock is going to go down in price. Maybe there was some bad news. Perhaps the industry is in trouble. Whatever the case may be, after research you figure out that the stock is going down.

Another source of information for short selling is when you see that there is a tremendous momentum downwards for a stock. You can then sell that stock short and ride that stock down, and later buy it long as it goes back up. This is actually how many traders make their money. They make money when the stock is going down, and they make money when the stock is going up.

Of course, it is a lot riskier to sell short because if the stock actually goes in the opposite direction, you have to cover your margin position. When you borrowed the stocks, you, in fact, borrowed on credit from the brokerage. When that stock appreciates in value instead of sinking, the brokerage will issue a margin call, and you would have to cover your position and buy it at a higher price and suffer a loss. That is the risk you take.

Margin Trading

Margin trading is simply trading using money you do not have. You borrow money from your brokerage based on a certain ratio. You then pay your brokerage a daily interest on that money you borrowed.

If you know what you are doing, you can actually make quite a bit of money on margin trading. Here is how it works. Compare these two scenarios. You have $1,000, and you use it to buy stocks. At the end of the day, the stocks are worth $2,000. Your profit when you liquidate your position is $1,000. That is how much you gained.

Now, what if you did not just use your own money? Instead, you used margin trading. You borrowed the stocks from the stock brokerage that you are using, and bought positions in them.

In this case, the maximum margin ratio used by many brokerages is 4:1. In this case, instead of just making $1,000, you can earn $4,000. Even if you were to take out the fee that you paid to borrow that money, you are still ahead by a lot more than if you only used your own money. This is why a lot of traders, especially day traders, use margin trading.

Of course, as you can probably already tell, this can be very dangerous. You are certainly playing with money you do not own. What if the stock went in the opposite direction? This is where you can get crushed. You have to sell at a loss as quickly as possible to minimize your losses. Margin trading may multiply the amount of money you make, but it can also multiply your losses if you are not careful.

Mutual Funds

Mutual funds are investment vehicles managed by a professional investor. That fund manager's job is simply to research stocks. That is what that person does all day every day. The fund manager would then buy many different stocks to diversify the risks in the fund, and the fund is offered to the general public. People acquire shares in the fund instead of buying stocks directly. The big advantage of investing this way is you are benefiting from the investment skills of the fund manager.

The downside to mutual funds is that they follow a diversification strategy. They do not just focus on one stock that may be appreciating very quickly. Instead, you are invested in a basket of stocks where some stocks may be going up by a lot while other stocks sink. At the end of the day, your mutual fund appreciates at a decent rate but not as much as if you were invested directly in hot stocks. You pay quite a bit of opportunity costs so you can get this level of protection.

The great thing about mutual funds, however, is that you do not have to worry. It is not your job to manage your stocks. You have a fund a manager for that.

The other downside to mutual funds is that you obviously have to pay a fee for this management, and usually the fund manager takes the fee from the total asset appreciation of the funds as a whole as well as fees allowed by law. Depending on the mutual fund you are invested in, this can add up to quite a bit of money. In a typical mutual fund, when you buy in or you sell your stake in the fund, you have to pay a fee. This is called a load.

No-Load Funds

No-load funds are mutual funds that do not charge you any money when you enter a position or when you leave your position. This is because your shares in that particular investment company are actually distributed directly to you. You do not have to go through an intermediary or middle person.

Front and Back-Loaded Funds

A front-loaded fund means that you have to pay money to invest in a particular mutual fund. This is above and beyond the investment that you are putting in. For example, if you are investing $20,000 into a fund, and they charge a 5% front-end load, this means that you will pay $1,000 just to invest your $20,000 in their fund.

In the same token, a back-end loaded fund simply means that you pay when you pull your money out. You do not pay any money coming in, but you pay the percentage when you are liquidating your position in that investment company.

Income Funds

Income funds are a type of mutual fund that exchange traded funds or any other investment vehicle, which earns money by investing only in securities like stocks or bonds that pay out a dividend or interest. In short, not only are you benefiting when the value of the stock the income fund invested in goes up, but you also benefit from the active income those stocks and bonds generate.

Management Expense Ratio

When you are investing in mutual funds, you need to pay attention to management expense ratio. This is expressed in a percentage form. This ratio measures how much of the total assets of the mutual fund you are thinking of buying into, goes into administrative management and other costs associated with running the mutual fund as well as marketing it.

For example, if the annual management expense ratio figure for the mutual fund you are considering comes out to 2%, that is how much of the fund's overall assets are used to pay for expenses. Now, it may seem like 2% is a small thing, but if you note that the mutual fund actually has assets over $5 billion, then you can see that 2% equals to $100 million. This is no small potato. One of the ongoing concerns investors have with mutual funds, especially giant mutual funds, is whether the expense ratio is justified.

How to Use a Brokerage to Trade

If you are considering trading online, you need to use an online brokerage. You just sign up for an account; they verify your account; and they give you instructions on how to fund your account. Usually, this involves a bank wire. Once there is money in your account, you can then access parts of the online brokerage that handles trading for you.

You can instruct the trading platform to buy stock of a company once that stock hits a certain price. This way, you can buy at a low price. You can then turn around and instruct the platform to sell your position once the stock hits a certain price. This way, you can be sleeping and still be confident that you have bought low, and you will sell high. That is how you make a profit when you are buying long.

Chapter 5 : Stock Trading Terms in Basic English (Part 2)

Limit Orders

A limit order is an order made on your brokerage platform's software where you instruct the brokerage to buy or sell stock at a certain price. For example, if you are buying and the price does not sync to the price that you want to buy at, then the order is not executed. Similarly, if you are trying to sell your stock and the price does not rise to where you wish to sell it, subsequently your order to sell is not executed. Limit orders, by definition, have a fixed time. It is usually good for the day. However, you can set up your limit order so that it can be in effect for a long time until the stock price hits the price point where you want to either buy or sell.

Limit Order Duration

A limit order can be valid only for the day, or it can be good until canceled. If you have placed a limit order to sell, for example, and you have set it at "good until canceled," then the investment brokerage platform will solely sell your stock if the stock price hits your target price. There is, however, a limit to good-until-canceled orders. It cannot go on forever. Many brokerages would restrict good-until-canceled limit orders to a few months maximum.

Trading Strategies

Trading strategies involve approaches to trading. Well, the main purpose of making money never changes. Your strategy differs based on a time frame. Some trading strategies focus on the actual value of the stock. They look at the fundamentals behind the stock. They look at the quality of the company, and then they buy in. It does not really matter whether they are buying high or buying low, as long as they get in the company because they are going to buy and hold the company for a long time.

Other trading strategies do not actually look at the quality of the stock. For many traders, they do not even look at the industry the company is in; they do not look at the news about the company. All they are looking at is the actual behavior of the stock price. They look at whether the stock is trending up or trending down. They would then quickly get in and get out of the stock to lock in a nice little profit. Day traders use this strategy.

There really is no right or wrong answer when it comes to trading strategies. You can make quite a bit of money either way. You can just quickly get in and get out, or you can hold for a long time. In fact, the most renowned investor, Warren Buffett, is famous for buying good companies and holding them for the long haul. When he exits a company, he exits with a nice profit. That is why he is a legendary investor.

It all depends on your goals, your risk appetite and your risk profile. It also depends on your timeline. Do you want to make a few thousand dollars a day or are you looking for a big payoff in the future? Do you need the money now or are you okay with cashing out big time in the future? It all depends on what your needs are.

Resistance Level

Resistance level is a term stock traders use for a certain price point that a stock cannot get past. For example, if you are trading a stock that ranges from $40 to $45 for the past couple of days, the $45 mark is the resistance level. It seems that once the stock moves from $40 all the way to $45, it has a tough time making it past that point. Resistance level is measured not just by the actual price of the stock, but investors also pay attention to the volume of the trades at certain price points. This is how they can make an educated guess as to whether a stock has the potential to break past the resistant level and go higher.

Support Level

The support level is the term stock traders use for the price at which a stock cannot sink beneath. For example, if you are trading a stock that ranges from $40 to $45, the support level is $40. You may have bought the stock at $42, and then it sank to $40. You can at least get some measure of comfort knowing that is the support level. That stock's price is going to have a tough time sinking beneath that because there are enough buyers to support it at the $40 level. Still, you are out $2 because you bought it at $42.

Regardless, this is much better than if the stock has a support level of $30, and you bought it at $42. I hope you can see how that works out. Usually, a stocks' resistance and support levels are factored in by the stock trader before the trader takes a position in that particular stock.

Stock Breakout

Breakout is the term used by stock traders to describe a situation where the price of the stock rises above its resistance level or crashes beneath its support level. Now, it is important to note that this is not just a simple observation of the price. Please note that for a breakout to occur, the surge past the resistance or the crash past the support must also be accompanied by higher trading volume.

When professional traders see this, they see a trend so what they do is when they see the stock breaking out past the resistance level, they would take a long position. They would buy long at slightly above the resistance level and try to ride the stock up and sell once it hits another resistance level.

By the same token, if they see the stock has crashed beneath the support level, they would sell the stock short near the support level, and they would ride the stock down until it hits another support level. The key here is volume. You have to pay attention to the volume; otherwise, you might buy in at the wrong time and end up stuck in your position.

Pullback

A pullback happens when a stock hits a high price point and then starts to sink from that high point. This can be a temporary reversal because after a few minutes or a few hours, the stock breaks past the high point to reach another high point and later pulls back again. It is important to pay attention to pullback if a stock is trending upwards. You can time your trade in such a way that you can buy a rising stock at a discount because you buy in at a pullback.

Swing Trading

Swing trading is a trading strategy where you trade based on longer-term changes in the price of the stock you invested in. The best way to define swing trading is to compare with day trading. A day trader enters and leaves a stock within a day or less than a day. They are in it for the short-term changes in the prices, whether going up or going down.

A swing trader, on the other hand, makes money on a short-term basis. We are talking as short as two days and as long as six days. This is the average. Some swing traders can go as long as two weeks.

Swing traders make money primarily on trends involving stocks that take some time to play out. Maybe there is heavy marked reaction to certain news about the stock, and the stock is going tremendously, and the swing trader hangs on for a long enough time to cash in on the rise because the stock might start facing resistance and start trending lower again. Similarly, a swing trader can also buy stock while at its high point under the impression that the stock will start to sink because of bad news or because of the simple fact that the stock is trending downward. In this case, the investor is simply riding the stock down.

IRA - Individual Retirement Accounts

In the US Tax Code, individuals are allowed to put away a certain amount of money every single year into their retirement fund. This is their IRA, an individual retirement account. The great benefit of such an account is that the money that you put in is not taxed. You can deduct this from the income you report to the IRS.

Furthermore, depending on the IRA you have set up, any money that your investment makes is not taxed at the time you of the appreciation. Instead, your IRA's appreciation is taxed when you are redeeming the account. This is called the Roth IRA. It is tax-free at the time of the trades but taxed when you are actually pulling out or redeeming your IRA.

Keep in mind that there are many different investments you can engage in with your IRA. You are not necessarily stuck with stock investment. You can invest in bonds. You can invest in gold or precious metals.

Chapter 6: Know the Importance of Trading Strategies

Now that you have a clear idea about the terms involved in stock trading, as well as a clear idea of your risk appetite and risk profile, we can then talk about trading strategies. As the old saying goes, "If you fail to plan, you are actually planning to fail." This cannot be any truer than when applied to stock trading. How bad can it get? Well, you can lose thousands, if not, hundreds of thousands of dollars if you do not have a clear, well-thought-out strategy.

Think of your strategy as both a map and a compass. It is too easy to get into trading and just do everything by impulse. You let your emotions get the better of you. You get swept in by all sorts of trading fads and heavily hyped stock alerts that are "a sure thing."

Well, let me tell you, if somebody could tell you how the market will trade tomorrow or at any point in the future, everybody would be a millionaire because those kinds of claims are a dime a dozen. It seems like everybody makes those claims, and unfortunately, individual traders have a very tough time making a living of stock trading because of these conflicting messages. They get all excited about a particular investment newsletter, and then they try it out; it does not pan out, subsequently they get excited about another investment system and on and on it goes. At the end of that journey, you have very little to show for all the time, effort, and yes, money you invested in stock trading.

It is important to begin trading stock with a strategy in mind. In other words, before you even begin trading your first penny's worth of stock, you have to have a strategy in place. Does this mean that you are wedded to the strategy for life? Absolutely not!

What this means, however, is that you at least are going to be trading in a systematic and methodical way. You are going to be trading with your eyes wide open and paying attention to all sorts of different factors. You are aware of the process; instead of just rushing from one hot stock or one trending stock to the other without really a clear idea of what you are doing and what your purpose is.

When you implement the different strategies that I outline below, you are essentially setting a map for yourself. Some people are looking for quick returns. They want to make thousands of dollars every single day. They want to make stock trading their livelihood. There are certain strategies that fit those needs.

Other people are looking simply to fight inflation. They just want to make sure that the money that they worked so hard to earn all these years maintains its value. There is a trading strategy for that.

For all other points in between, you have to focus on what your needs are and also your risk profile and appetite. Everything has to square with the particular trading strategy that you are using. For example, if you are in your 60s, it is probably a bad idea to get into day trading. You can lose your shirt and unlike a person who is in her early 20s, you most likely will not have as much time to get that money back. You cannot earn that money back because you are almost a few years away from retirement, or you have already retired.

You always have to factor in your risk profile as well as your risk appetite along with your needs. Sure, everybody can appreciate making several thousand dollars a day. Who would not? The problem is we may not have the proper profile for the strategies that give us a shot at making that kind of money through trading stocks. So, it is really important at this stage when selecting among different strategies to focus on how much capital you have, what year needs are, as well as your risk profile and appetite.

How Strategies Impact your Bottom Line

Your choice of strategy plays a big role in how you measure success. A day trader, for example, can call it a victory if he or she walks away with a $500 to $1,000-dollar gain every single day. That is a big deal to the day trader. Other people are looking for something more long term. The success they see for themselves is buying Apple at $100 per share and selling it at $250 a share. The strategy you select impacts how you measure your success.

Always Focus on ROI

Let me let you in on a secret. The first trading strategy that you are going to implement when you start trading is probably not going to be the strategy that you are going to stick over the long haul. Why? This is a learning process. What seemed like a good fit in the beginning might not be all that applicable. Something that may have seemed really wild to you or something that does not fit your profile might actually be the better choice. Unfortunately, the only way to figure out which strategy is best for you is really to try one strategy after the other.

How do you know when it is time to switch out from one strategy to an alternative one? Very simple. Keep a laser focus on your ROI. Pay attention to the amount of time you put into trading as well as your actual profits.

As I have mentioned in the definition section of this book, ROI is calculated both in terms of overall gains (this is the profit that you make) and the time involved. You are always going to divide the profit by the amount of time. This is your adjusted ROI factoring in time. Think of it this way. It is really easy to get excited when you hear that somebody made 100% ROI. In other words, they invested 10,000, and they got 20,000. Sounds awesome, right? What is not to love, right?

Well, what if it took them 30 years to get that return? That is ridiculous! That is ridiculously low compared to other ROI you could have otherwise enjoyed pursuing other investment opportunities in the stock market. Do you see how this works? You could have adopted a trading strategy and blown away that ROI over that ridiculously long period of time.

Let ROI be your North Star or guiding light when it comes to figuring out the best stock trading strategy. Again, the strategy that may seem so appealing right now may not practically be a good idea. Similarly, an investment strategy that may seem quite risky or may seem a bit too technical for you may actually be the strategy that you would do best with. You will only know once you implement.

Your job right now is actually quite simple. Know when to quit a strategy and switch to a new one. We are not talking about making thousands upon thousands of dollars a day. We are not talking about striking it rich and buying yourself a new Ferrari.

Our ambition is actually pretty straightforward and very limited yet realistic and positions you for great success in the future. The bottom line is you should focus on learning right now while minimizing your losses. Make no mistake about it, if you do not know what you are doing, the learning process can be a very expensive experience.

Your job right now is to learn as quickly as possible. Put simply, learn how to fail hastily at minimal cost. This is really important because a lot of people get all excited about figuring out what to do. The way life actually turns out is that you can also focus on learning what not to do.

They both lead you to the same place. So, do yourself a big favor and either fail quickly but cheaply or be very clear on what you are looking for and pay attention to what you are doing and your return on investment, so you can eventually adopt the right trading strategy for you.

Basic Trading Strategies

Here are the four basic trading strategies that you should look into. They all involve subsidiary strategies. There is a lot of confusion regarding these strategies because a lot of people use different labels for them, but I have simplified them as much as possible into four different types. Many of these come under fancy names, but focus on what you are actually doing. That is how I have classified these strategies to make them as clear as possible.

It is also important to understand that regardless of the strategy that you employ; in addition, you have to do proper analysis. Analysis is what will make or break these strategies. These strategies can help you achieve your financial goals on a day-to-day basis or a long-term basis only if you do the proper analysis.

There are two types of stock analysis. There are the fundamental and technical analyses. I will go into that in the next chapter but in this chapter, I am just going to walk you through the four basic trading strategies.

Swing Trading

Swing trading involves buying stock in a company and waiting between two to six days to a couple of weeks for that stock to reach its full potential. By full potential, I am not necessarily talking about the stock going up. If you are short selling the stock, its fullest potential for you, at least, is when it crashes to a very low level. Once it reaches a target point, you then exit the stock. Swing traders normally put in a good-until-canceled order.

For example, based on technical analysis, a stock is showing a lot of volume, and it is meeting a lot of resistance at 30. Based on volume analysis, it seems like people are buying more and more into the stock, and the volume is increasing tremendously. In this situation, I would then put in a good-until-canceled buy limit order for any price above $30. Sure enough, a lot more investors plow into the stock, and the stock goes past the $30 resistance level, and I lock at $30.25. It then hits $31 and there is a pullback to $29.

A swing trader would wait several days or even a couple of weeks until the stock reaches a profitable point or to maximize opportunity costs; the trader leaves the stock at a slight loss. Whatever the case may be, swing trading involves taking a position only to the point where the stock reaches your target appreciation and you automatically exit. Swing traders can utilize technical stock analysis using volume and price fluctuations, or they can employ stock value analysis by paying attention to things like the revenue of the company, competitive position, industry position as well as prospective developments in the news that might impact the company's stock performance. Regardless of the analysis that they used, swing traders pursue a strategy where they will remain parked in the stock for enough time to see a nice swing up or a nice swing down.

Position Trading

A position trader is somebody who will buy a position in a company for the long term. By long term, we are talking about several months to even years. The position trader is not really worried about the short-term fluctuations of the stock. This type of strategy does not rely on trends or market fluctuations in terms of the company's particular evaluation. Instead, the position trader uses a strategy that smooths out whatever near-term price volatility may be. The key to success in position trading is a fairly long-term yet steady rate of appreciation.

For example, if your end goal is to protect your money's value against inflation and taxes, then your strategy would be to take the rate of inflation as well as your desired growth rate and use that as your ROI benchmark. You do this, of course, with the understanding that taxes will be taken up. So, a position trader then would look at the beginning the year when they bought the position and at the end of the year where they are still hanging on to the stock. If they see that there is a nice percentage increase in ROI, compared to inflation and other factors; afterward, they consider their trade successful.

Usually, position traders would not just measure their success against inflation because, let us face it, for the past decade, inflation has been very, very low. In fact, it is abnormally inferior by historical standards. It is so low that it is kind of scary if you ask me.

Instead, the position trader would factor in opportunity costs. An opportunity cost is obviously defined as the value of alternative investments. Put simply, if you did not invest in this stock and chose to invest in another stock instead, how would your current stock measure up? That is when you know whether you left a lot of money on the table, or you are actually doing quite well because alternative stocks are not doing that great. Position traders use the Dow Jones Industrial index or some sort of index to determine the relative health of their portfolio. If they notice that the rate of appreciation of their portfolio keeps up with the rest of the market, then they consider themselves successful.

Day Trading

Day trading is actually not even stock investing. If you are going to be completely honest about it, day trading is simply looking at technical signals or use related developments that impact a stock. For example, when your stock research software tells you in real time that a huge amount of investors are just plowing into a stock, then this should give you a good idea that something is about to break lose. People are buying into the stock in very high volumes. What you would do then is take a position based on a resistance level and if the stock breaks past that resistance level, you lock into your position. You subsequently ride up the upward momentum made possible by the increasing volume of trades in that stock.

Now, keep in mind that this goes the other way as well. If your stock research software notifies you that a stock is being traded heavily and there is a heavy volume in sales, this is going to put a tremendous downward pressure on the stock. You then take a position at a certain support level and once that support level is breached; you lock in for a purchase, and you ride the stock down. Once it bottoms out, you later buy back your shares that you have sold short.

Day trading involves very brief periods of time. We are talking a day or less than a day. In fact, a lot of day traders are quickly in and out of a stock in a matter of hours. Given the fact that they trade in volume due to margin accounts, they can make quite a nice chunk of money by simply trading a small proportion or even half a percent movement in certain stocks.

Again, the whole point in day trading is not looking the stock and analyzing its industry significance, its future prospects, new products, industry positioning, so on and so forth. No. Day trading is all about looking at technical trading characteristics and making a judgment call as to where the market is going regarding certain stocks. You then lock in a position and afterward you either ride up the stock, or you ride it down.

Value Investing

Value investing is also known as the Warren Buffett strategy or buy and hold. Value investing boils down to buying stock that the market has somehow someway overlooked. What you are actually doing is you are looking at a company that is in a really good position and should be valued more by the stock market. For whatever reason, its stock price is, in your opinion, below its full value in the future.

This is how Warren Buffet became a multibillionaire many times over. He has this uncanny ability of looking at certain companies that may be trading at a very high price already but looking at their balance sheet as well as their industry positioning and the health of the US or global economy several years down the road, and using these pieces of information to make stock purchase decisions. Obviously, he is doing something right because he has become one of the wealthiest people on the planet using this strategy.

It is important to understand that value investing does not necessarily mean you buy a company which has a stock price that seems stuck. Ideally, that would be the best. However, value investing also means paying top dollar for a company that is trading at a decent level now with the confidence that price is actually going to go much higher in the future. You then buy the stock, and you hold onto it for a long period of time. Your success meter factors in several years of appreciation.

As you can already tell, swing trading and day trading tend to go hand in hand. Position trading and value investing tend to go hand in hand as well. These four strategies differ from each other, but these two pairings involve quite a bit of similarity. Again, when picking a trading strategy, make sure you factor in what makes sense to you, your needs, your immediate and midterm financial goals as well as your risk appetite and risk profile.

Chapter 7: Swing Trading

Swing trading is a trading strategy that uses technical information or news analysis to plan and execute one's trades. It's important to note that you can either use publicly released news information regarding a particular stock or you can use technical analysis. The key differentiating factor to swing trading is that you hang on for several days or a couple of weeks, unlike day trading, which requires you to basically get in and get out of the stock within the day and not a minute over.

The reason why day traders need to leave within the day is because in many cases, stocks move in price over night. They may have traded at a certain price when the market closed the previous day, but when the market opens the other day, the stock might open much higher or much lower. This is too much risk for day traders since they are often heavily leveraged. They have borrowed a tremendous amount of money to increase the magnitude of their earnings.

This also increases their risk tremendously. It's so risky that they cannot essentially park a stock overnight. It's too much risk. While it would be nice if the stock opens higher than it closed before, it's just as likely that when the stock opens, it opens below its previous close, and whatever money the day trader makes is vaporized.

The swing trader doesn't trade within a day. The swing trading strategy involves buying a stock and waiting for quite some time. This can range from two days to a couple of weeks or more. The whole point of swing trading is to make money when the stock breaks out. This is a point where the stock gets past its resistance level and keeps going up.

Usually, swing traders would target a particular appreciation rate like, let's say, 10%. Once the stock reaches that rate of return, the swing trader would liquidate his or her total position. Another way to swing trade is to liquidate your position gradually. For example, if you are sure that the stock is going to appreciate quite dramatically, then you can set up your trades so that you can sell half your holdings when the stock reaches a 10% gain.

At this point, there was a breakout that occurred. However, you keep the remaining 50% of your holdings and schedule 25% liquidation, and the stock appreciates another 5%, and so on and so forth. This way, swing traders have already locked in their gains with the first breakout.

However, since you really can't tell just how much higher a stock can breakout by using a graduated liquidation strategy, you increase the chances that you would make more money. Put simply, you position yourself to benefit as much as possible from the breakout in trading.

Dealing with Pullbacks

It would be nice if a stock broke out and just went one direction. It would be nice if a stock broke past the certain price point and just kept rising and rising. Well, even if we're talking about Apple computers or any other historically fast rising stock, there are days where it suffers a loss. This is called the pullback, and swing traders can also make money with pullbacks.

They basically liquidate on a high point and then set aside a certain percentage of their capital to scoop up the stock if it dips past the certain point. Whether we're looking at breakouts or pullbacks, you're going to still use the same analysis. You're going to pay attention to the following factors to spot if a stock is either going to breakout or if it's going to pullback, how much of pullback will it suffer, and at what price point should you buy. Here are the factors that you should look at.

Bullish Trend

By looking at the volume of a stock and its price appreciation, you can tell that there is a tremendous demand for the stock, but the price hasn't really responded tremendously. Pay attention to volume. This speaks quite loudly regarding investor sentiment. If you noticed that there's a lot more buying than selling, but the price seems to move very slowly, this means that there is a tremendous upward pressure.

Any small changes in the resistance to upward pressures might release the stocks from its sluggish appreciation and you may not see a nice percentage gain over several days. Look for that bullish trend. The stock must be on a definite upward swing. It doesn't have to be very pronounced, but as long as you can see the incremental rise of the stock with ever increasing volumes, then you know that something is about to blow up.

Stock Selling under Resistance

If you notice that the stock sells below the resistance level, but the resistance price seems to be stuck for a long time, this is a key indicator of a potential breakout. It seems like the people are selling, but the price doesn't really drop dramatically. In fact, it remains stuck. Regardless of how much stock was sold, there's still more than enough buyer interest to keep the resistance fairly stable.

Resistance seems Stuck for a long time

This is one key indicator you should look for. If you notice that the stock is appreciating by small increments but seems to basically be stuck within a particular range for a very long time while volume is increasing, this is a key indicator that if some slight changes happens, there is a higher chance that the stock will spike up rather than dip down.

Increasing Trade Volume with Little Price Change

I can't repeat this enough. If you notice that there is an increased level of buying activity while the price doesn't change, pay close attention. This means that there is a tremendous buyer interest and the price seems stuck. If the selling side of the pricing equation finally slows down, expect the stock to break out. This should not be all that surprising because of the tremendous buying pressure.

Risks associated with Swing Trading

There are risks with swing trading. First of all, your money is going to be parked in stock for quite some time. This is painfully obvious if you are a day trader. As a day trader, you're normally most comfortable with quick in and out trades. Not so with swing trading. You basically have to content yourself with camping out on the stock for an extended period of time.

This can be very risky on two fronts. First of all, you could simply make the wrong bet. The stock that you thought poised for a breakout simply just sits there. This is actually the worst thing that can happen. If you think about it, this is worse than the stock depreciating. Why?

You're forced to wait and wait and wait. In the meantime, you're not using your capital to make money with quick gains playing other stocks. This can be very problematic. The second risk that you take is the opportunity cost because you cannot split up your trades in so many ways to diversify your risk. You need a large pool of capital to make your swing trade worthwhile. And since you're not able to do those diverse trades, you might possibly be losing out big time.

How do you Make Money when a Stock Pulls Back and Rises?

Swing trading works both ways. You can make money from breakout swing trades. You can also make money from pullback swings. When a stock pulls back, you sell when the stock hits your target price and then you wait for any pullback. You then buy at the bottom of the pullback and then you wait until the stock swings up again, then you unload, then you keep repeating this process.

If you play your cards right, you can make a tremendous amount of money in a fairly short period of time. Still, that length of time can still seem too long for people who normally day trade. So how can you tell if a stock is right for a pullback swing? Pay attention to the following factors. It rows previously.

The first thing that you need to look at is the fact that the stock hit a high point previously. This is really important. Make sure that it has already hit a high point. It's very hard to predict a pullback when the stock is still rising. If you're in a middle of a rising stock, it's going to be hard to do a pullback strategy.

The Pullback is Recent

Now that you've found a stock that had a nice high point and then has pulled back, pay attention to how long it's been since the stock pulled back. You need to look for a recent pullback, not a pullback that happened six months ago.

You know that you're in a slow moving stock if the pullback actually happened several months ago. Look for a stock that just suffered a recent pullback. Maybe less than a week, or a week, or two. It's also important to make sure that the pull back is less than 50% of the total value of the stock.

For example, if you are thinking of doing a pullback swing strategy trading on a stock that peak that $100, it's a good idea to make sure that the pullback was fairly recent and the price that you're going to buy into is not less than 50% of the $100. In this case, $50.

If the stock is trading at $30 and it just crashed from $100 peak, you might want to hold off. That stock might still have ways to fall. But if you noticed that the pullback was fairly recent but it didn't fall below 50%, then you may be able to play that stock.

Lower Volume during Sell Off than Appreciation

This is the smoking gun. If this factor is present in the trading performance of the stock you are considering for a pullback trade, you're in luck because this speaks volumes as to the investor demand for that stock. If the stock's price fell based on fairly low volume compared to how much of the stock was being bought when it was on its way up. This is a clear indicator that there's still a lot of buyer sentiment in that stock.

Pay Attention to other Strength Signals

It's important to note that when you're doing pullback swing trading, you also have to pay attention to value fundamentals. This is really important because you can't just rely on technical information like volume and incremental appreciation, or incremental declines in the prices. The reason why you're doing quite a bit of value or fundamental analysis is because you want to make sure that the stock will pull back. While you really cannot be sure if its fundamentals are quite solid, there's a higher and even chance that the stock will recover.

What factors should you look at? Well, pay attention to price per earnings ratio or PE ratio. Pay attention to the fundamental details of the company. What industry is it in? Is its industry on the upswing? Is it a market leader?

Also, pay attention to its stock performance compared to the rest of the market. If everything lines up, then the stock that suffered a recent price decline might actually be a good candidate for a pullback swing. Again, you have a window of two days to two weeks for your investment to hit its targets before you leave the stock.

Don't be afraid to leave a stock if you're doing swing trading. This is really important. This is a very important piece of advice. Why? It's all about opportunity costs. If you just suffered a fairly small, like maybe 3% to 5% loss, that's fine. Call it a day. Why? You probably would be better off playing another stock that has a higher chance of delivering what you're looking for. In other words, a stock that can appreciate significantly during your swing trade cycle. This is a key rule to swing trading.

Do not be afraid to cut your losses. Do not be afraid to cut and run. If you become emotionally invested in your position, you might remain stuck in that position for a long time, and the stock really goes nowhere. You made a bad swing trade because the stock never really swung.

I hope that much is clear so please do not find yourself stuck at a stock because you got emotionally attached or you felt that you've invested so much time and energy already. You need to learn how to cut your losses and start fresh again with another stock and try to ride that stock up.

Chapter 8: Day Trading

Day trading has been popular for quite some time. The whole point of day trading is to get in and out of a stock as quickly as possible. While contrary to what the name indicates, a lot of day traders actually take less than a day, or eight hours to trade.

In many cases, they would take one or two hours, and they're done. Day trading is really all about locking in fairly small incremental gains. Normally, when people look at a gain of 1% or half a percent, people might think that that's really insignificant. Many investors might think that it's really insignificant. Indeed, a large number of investors would insist that they would hang on to their position, at least for a long enough time, for them to make more than one or a couple percent profit.

Believe it or not, that 1% or 2% gain is big enough for a day trader. A day trader is not of the same mindset as Warren Buffett who is looking to buy really valuable companies that will continue to grow in value over time. They really couldn't care less about long term value. In fact, day trading is not investing at all. It has nothing to do with investing. Instead, you're simply focusing on the movement of the stock.

As long as there is some sort of microscopic gain per share, you lock in and count your gain. That's how day trading works. Now, you may be asking if a stock appreciated by half a percent or a percent or two percent, at the end of the day, that's really that much money, especially if we're talking about a fairly low priced stock.

Well, keep in mind that day traders trade on margin. In other words, they multiply the amount of capital they have available to them by taking out a short term loan from their brokerage account. Even if the stock gained only half a percent or one percent, thanks to the large volume of stocks made possible by margin trading, a day trader can actually come out with a fairly nice chunk of cash. It all depends on volume.

The secret to day trading is speed. The day trader would use a high speed trading platform to zero in on gains when a stock makes a small incremental gain of half a percent, one percent, or two percent. Day traders use high speed trading platforms to make sure that once the price of the stock hits a certain threshold, they exit the stock immediately.

Paired with large margin accounts, this can translate to a nice payday every single day. It's not uncommon for day traders to make thousands, if not tens of thousands of dollars every day. Institutional day traders, on the other hand stand, to gain millions of dollars because of the huge amount of capital that they are working with. Regardless of the size of your capital, you can make quite a bit of money with day trading provided you diversify.

The Importance of Diversification

Expert day traders don't just trade one stock. They know that in many cases, the stock might actually be trading sideways so they'd be lucky if they get half a percent or a quarter of a percent. To maximize their gains, they would play many different stocks and each of them has their own microscopic target of price appreciation. It's not uncommon for a day trader to set a 1% gain across many different stocks. This might seem like a waste of time, but when you look at how much cash was involved and how much volume, this can result in a fairly nice chunk of cash

Risks of Day Trading

The problem with day trading is you really can't afford to take a position that lasts past a day because there might be large price movements from the time the market closed the day before to the time the market closed the next day. This price change can wipe out your gains.

Since you are trading on margin, you might end up in a lot of debt. This is how a lot of traders get into trouble. They are so leveraged that one false move, as far as day to day or overnight price changes go, can totally wipe them out. We're not just talking about wiping out your profits. We're also talking about just completely wiping you out because you'll be in debt. That's how bad things could be.

Not surprisingly, day traders stick to trading within the day. Like I said, some would prefer to trade one or two hours and they're done. Another key risk here, just in case it isn't painfully obvious, is the fact that for you to make any sort of real money with day trading, you have to borrow. You take your 10, 000 and you turn it into forty 40, 000 so when you make incremental gains of that 40, 000, the gains translate to real money.

Now, the problem is if you were to stick to the cash that you have, your small gains will indeed be very microscopic because you don't have the scale. The problem with scaling up by taking our credit with your brokerage account is that the market can easily turn against you and you can get wiped out. It's really important when you're doing day trading to make sure you have limit sell orders to establish a bottom for your positions.

What I mean by this is you lock in a price at which you will sell, so if you're waiting for the stock to go up but it actually reverses course and goes the other direction, you're protected because your price floor kicks in and you don't lose as much money as you could have otherwise. This is another key lesson of day trading. While it's easy to see the upside for the most part, it's also a game of trying to minimize your losses as you try to look for a breakout trade.

Chapter 9: Position Trading

Position trading is when you hang on to a stock for several weeks or even months. Position traders hang on for a longer period than swing traders. You are more focused on a longer term game plan and you're confident that the gains that you would accomplish with such a longer timeline are going to be higher than if you tried other strategies. The biggest factors for position trading involve three elements: news trends, earnings cycle, and industry trends.

News Trends

Traders who use a position trading strategy essentially invest in the stock. The fact that they're digging in for up to several months shows that they're investing in the value of the stock being appreciated by the broader market.

One of the main factors that they base this strategy on is the news involving the particular stock. Maybe there's some sort of drug application approval that's spending. Maybe there's some sort of a new patent or program that was launched. Whatever the case may be, there is an event that was made known to the public, and there is some sort of a cut off in the future regarding a decision on that event.

For example, a biotechnology company may have been developing a breakthrough cancer drug for several years. All that time, the stock may have been going up and down or trading sideways. A position trader would take a position on that stock if there was news that within a few weeks or a few months, there would be an FDA decision regarding its drug application.

Now, what makes many biotechnology stocks fairly good position plays is the fact that they are fairly predictable in terms of their news cycles. In the United States, for new medication to be approved by the FDA, there has to be some several phases in the drug application. There are the lab trials, the clinical trials, and the formal application. Each of these news events can be points in time where the position trader can buy into the company.

Using the biotechnology example once again, if a company is working on an anti-cancer drug, they would first announce that their lab results indicate that they have a promising compound. When the news comes out, this can be a buying opportunity. However, it's anybody's guess whether this seemingly promising technology would really pan out, as far as commercialization is concerned, because the drug still has to go from internal laboratory testing, to wider lab testing, to human clinical trials, and then formal application.

A position trader can take a position on the stock and wait until the next phase comes. Usually, they would wait until that point in time where clinical trials look so promising, that the company can then file a formal application. The stock can move quite a bit once a formal application is tendered by the company.

Can you imagine the effect on the stock when the FDA finally approves the application? So the key point here is there are fairly well-defined milestones for a biotechnology company's proposed drug to get approved. Position traders can look at the milestones and take positions accordingly. It's not uncommon for traders who specialize in biotechnology stocks to enter and leave a biotech stock several times as the company moves closer and closer to drug approval.

Other news trends to look out for involve strategic partnerships. For example, a company has just partnered with a large retail or pharmaceutical chain spread throughout the United States. Such deals and business developments can have a very positive material impact on a company's sales figures.

The position trader would then look at the announcement and then buy into the company based on the projected timeline of when the results of that static partnership will be released. Depending on how big the deal is, the position trader can actually make quite a bit of money if the distribution deal of the business alliance has a fairly significant impact on the company's bottom line.

Earnings Cycle

Another fairly predictable milestone or series of events position traders take advantage of are earnings cycles. When a company is about to announce its earnings in a month, a position trader would look at previous news releases to see if there is a positive trend here, or if there is a negative trend. Either way, the position trader would take up a position.

In the case of a positive trend, the position trader would buy long. In terms of negative trends, the trader would sell short. Whatever the case may be, there is a fairly short and predictable period of time between the time the trader took up a position and when the earnings event comes. Either the company made more money or made less money, the event will come, and the position trader can then liquidate his or her position.

It's important to note that there's a little bit of complication. Wall Street has evolved to the point that if a company manages to meet expectations, that may not be enough in of itself to boost the company's stock. In many cases, Wall Street expects companies to beat street expectations to gain a nice boost up.

For example, if Facebook announced that they are going to be making a dollar share and Facebook comes in at exactly a dollar share, chances are that performance was already factored into the stock price of Facebook by the time its next earnings cycle milestone comes up.

Now, compare this with Facebook announcing that it made a $1.25 profit per share. Assuming that the consensus expectation was $1 per share, this makes for tremendous news. A position trader that bought before the earnings cycle stands to gain a lot of money due to the fact that the company beat expectations. Always factor in the power of street expectations when it comes to the earnings cycle.

Don't be surprised if you take a long position several weeks before the earnings cycle plays out, and only for your stock to remain the same price or to even decline. Pay attention to street expectations. It is not uncommon for stocks to hit their announced earnings target and still see their stock price sink. Why? Wall Street was expecting the company to beat expectations. Simply coming in to meet expectations is not enough.

If you think that's bad, it's especially worse if the company misses expectations. If for example, Amazon stock was expected to earn a dollar per share, but the actual figure is 90 cents per share, this can put a tremendous downward pressure on the stock. Always factor in expectations.

Industry Trends

Another big factor in position trading involves industry trends. If you noticed that an industry, as a whole is poised for a breakout, then you can take a position in leading companies in that industry. It all depends on whether this industry breakout or recovery is factored into the prices of the stock price of the biggest companies in that industry.

The key to playing industry trends is not to buy the giant players in that industry. Chances are whatever appreciation you get would be quite incremental because everybody's paying attention to those companies. A lot of people are playing those companies. Whatever upward movement in your positions may be would basically be diluted by the huge number of people buying and selling that stock.

Instead, look for mid-tier companies that have a track record of appreciating quite well during industry recoveries. Alternatively, you can take positions in growth stocks within that industry. The reason why you should pursue this strategy is that the weight of return to your position would probably be much higher compared to you betting on the biggest players in that industry you're tracking.

You have to understand the biggest players in any industry are usually already bought into by big mutual funds and pension funds. In short, their institutional coverage is very high so they really have to outperform the industry tremendously for their stocks to get a nice lift up. This is not the case with middle tier or up and coming companies within that industry. These companies' stock prices can benefit tremendously if there is any sort of positive industry trend.

Risks in Position Trading

The biggest risk that you undertake when doing position trading doesn't involve your stock going down. Okay, let's just get that out of the way. Even if your stock were to tank, you should have a stop limit order on your stocks. Meaning, you decide for yourself going in what is the most you can afford to lose. You then put a stop limit sell order on that price.

For example, you buy into a stock that's worth $20. You then arrive at 10% as the maximum you're willing to lose on that position. Accordingly, if the stock ever dips down to $18, you will automatically neutralize your position. You will liquidate. You are completely out of the stock. This is how you protect yourself from your long position going south.

Believe me, this happens quite a bit. It doesn't happen all the time, but it does happen so you need to protect yourself. At least, you only lost at least 10%. You can then play the market again to recover. Also, keep in mind that when you lose money in stock trades, you can use that loss as an offset regarding any gains in the future. Still, the biggest worry you'll have when using a position trading strategy to stocks is that the stocks really don't go anywhere.

If you think about it, it may actually even be a good thing if the stock just sinks. Because once it sinks, you have set up your stop limit order so that you are out of that stock. It just didn't pan out. The worst thing that can happen is for the stock to essentially track sideways. For example, if you buy a company that is worth $20 share and for the whole year, you took a position and the price of the company basically went from $20, to $19, to $21, and never really varied. Why is this a problem?

Well, the problem here is your money is not growing so you're not beating inflation. Second, you're paying a huge amount of money in the form of opportunity costs. Can you imagine if you were to have not invested in that stock in the first place and traded another stock that is volatile enough for you to lock in a sizable profit? Which position would you rather be in?

You better believe that the opportunity cost in position trading can be quite huge. This is why a lot of position traders diversify their long positions. They know that out of a basket of stocks, some would sink so they would immediately liquidate their position. Others would track sideways, and while others would appreciate. What they would do then is to minimize the amount of stocks that would trade sideways. This way, a lot of your money is reserved for stocks that appreciate.

Always pay attention to the turnover of your capital because the timeframe might be so long that it turns out that it was really not worth your time and energy to have gotten into that stock at all. While the stock might appreciate a couple of percent here and there, you're looking for a fairly substantial return to fully recoup and make up for whatever opportunity costs you suffered.

This is the key to position trading. Make sure that the gain you got compensates or more than compensates for the amount of time you waited for the stock to appreciate.

Chapter 10: Value Investing

Value investing or fundamental investing is also known as the Warren Buffett school of investing. Warren Buffett, as I mentioned in a previous chapter, is a world famous investor. He lives in Omaha, Nebraska and this man is responsible for growing his investors' money several thousand times. I'm not saying that his stocks are worth several thousand dollars, I'm talking several thousand percent appreciation. That's how awesome of an investor Warren Buffet is.

The interesting thing about his investing style is he really doesn't pay attention to what the current price of the company is. Instead, he looks at long term value. It may well turn out that the stock of a company seems fairly high by today's standards. However, to Buffett, the stock is actually cheap in light of its future value.

The secret to value investing is future value. You basically would have to look at the track record of the company, its current operations and health, as well as the health of the industry it's in. You then project this information in the future factoring in potential future conditions. Once you have a fairly clear picture, you then buy in, and it's important to note that you basically don't leave. That's the whole point of value investing.

You buy and you hold. You're playing the long game. This strategy is strictly for people who buy long. Now, fresh from our discussion about position trading, you might be asking yourself, well if I buy long then I might be suffering opportunity cost because I could have been making more money in the short term buying a more volatile stock?

Believe me, if you play the biotech or internet stocks, they can be quite volatile. It's not uncommon for traders to make thousands of dollars every single day of volatility of these stocks. They move that quickly. Warren Buffett doesn't care about any of that. Instead, his game is to basically hold the company for several years or even decades and at the end of that long period, the stock has split many times or has gone up in value so much.

If you ever need proof of this, look at his main investment vehicle Berkshire Hathaway. Can you imagine if you have bought Berkshire Hathaway in the 80s? You would be a millionaire many times over today. That's how awesome of an investor Warren Buffet is. He's all about the long game. He's all about patient investing.

Now, value investing may not fit your investment goals. If your immediate goal is to have your money appreciate by 10% or 15% per year, value investing may not be a slam dunk. You have to understand that value investing looks at growth over time. It may be substantial growth. We're talking about the may be company's stock price doubling or even tripling, but it's anybody's guess when this will exactly happen.

It's not uncommon for a stock to only appreciate 5% the next year, and then the year after that goes up to 20%, and then dips down to 10%, so on and so forth. But when you average everything out, it turns out that the stock has actually doubled, tripled, or even quadrupled in price.

How to do Value Investing

Warren Buffett is known for simply reading the financial statements of a company, as well as their financial papers in the comfort of his office. He would then make phone calls to make million dollar stock purchases. That's all he does. He usually never goes to the actual company. He usually never reads the paper or checks out the news regarding the company.

All he pays attention to are their numbers. I don't expect you to master the game so well that you only need to see numbers. This is why you need to pay attention to the following factors.

Focus on CASH FLOW

Solid companies have cash flow volumes that justify their price. The company must be generating revenue. Even if it is no earning a profit, it must have enough cash flow to justify its price either now or some point in the future. Depending on how speculative the stock is, cash flow is determined by either P/E or price-to-book.

(P/E) Price to Earnings Ratio: The company's earnings per share is cross referenced to its current stock price. For example: if a company is earning $1 per share is trading at $20 per share, its P/E ratio is 20. This is an indication of cash flow value in reference to its current price. If you're going to use P/E as your cash flow factor, you should compare different stocks that have the same fundamentals (industry positioning, book value, growth factors, and others).

Price to book Ratio: After reading a company's balance sheet, you will be aware of all the assets a company has. After proper depreciation and discounting, whatever amount left is the liquidation value of the company's assets. In other words, if you were going to liquidate the company and get cash for all assets and you take out whatever debt the company owes, what's left is its book value. Price to book is the ratio of how many times the company's book value is multiplied to produce its current per share value. For example: if you have company that has a book value of $10 per share and it trades for $100 per share, it's price to book value is 10.

Please note that there are many other cash flow-based value calculation methods but P/E and price to book are the most common and are enough to guide any beginner investor. As you become more proficient at trading, you might want to scale up using other methods at calculating cash flow.

Focus on Industry Leaders

The first thing you need to do is to look for industry leaders or potential leaders in an industry. It's important to look at solid companies. These companies are doing something right. They're making money. They have made an impact. They've got their act together. It's important to focus on these qualities.

The problem with a lot of stock out there is that a lot of them are sold based on hype and potential. For example, Twitter traded as high as the low 40s because people are optimistic that somehow, someway, it's going to make money. Its valuation wasn't really based on how the company was run, how much money it was making, its position in the industry. None of that matter. All the focus was on potential growth.

Not so with value investing. You look at the actual position of the company and the fact that it is already making money. You start with that fact. The company has to be already well positioned. This doesn't mean that the company has already dominated its industry or is the number one player. It can be an up and comer. What's important is that it has its house in order.

It must have Solid Financials

A key indicator that a company has its financial house in order is that it has zero to low debt. A company that has almost no debt and a low stock price is actually quite underpriced. This is the kind of combination that Warren Buffett gets excited about. He knows that chances are quite good that for some reason or other, the market simply is not acknowledging the solid fundamentals of a company. And one key factor in that is its debt exposure.

If the company has almost zero debt and a low stock price and a solid market or industry presence, then the company has a good chance of being a good value investment. However, you need to look at other factors as well.

The Company is in a Growing Industry

Now, can you imagine doing your research in stocks and finding a company that is a soon to be industry leader, or is already an industry leader and has zero debt. It is also very profitable currently. On top of all of this, its stock is fairly low as measured by price per earnings ratio (P/E). Sounds like a slam dunk, right?

Well, hold your horses. Pay attention to the company that industry is in. It may well turn out that that company is the only gem in that industry because that industry is basically going downhill. In that situation, that company is probably going to have a bleak future. Its stock price might look good now, but it's only a matter of time until that company implodes or has to reinvent itself and enter another industry.

Pay attention to the industry. Is it under a tremendous amount of disruption? Or is it still a growing industry? The problem with industries that are under a tremendous amount of disruption is that you really don't know the direction the industry would go.

For example, the Eastman Kodak Corporation was the top dog of the photographic materials industry. Thanks to the rise of digital cameras, the photographic material industry is a shadow of its former self. It still exists in a very limited form, but it's definitely not big enough to sustain a company that's as gigantic as the Eastman Kodak.

Do you see how this works? And the problem was that the industry that was under serious disruption during the 90s and early 2000s. Steer clear from companies that are under disruption because it's anybody's guess what the ultimate direction of the technology or business strategies of the companies in that industry.

Heavy Cash Flow and large Cash Position

Another factor value investors look at is how much cash a company has on its book. Now, this is the key indicator of how well that company is run. If a company is profitable but it essentially just burns up its remaining cash on research and development, the company might not be a solid value investment because it's essentially spending a lot of money to make a lot of money.

Ultimately, it's basically just trying to tread water. This is not always the case. It also depends on the industry. Still, if you notice that a company has a lot of cash in its balance sheet and almost zero debt, that company is doing something right and if you can see that the cash at hand is growing over time, then this is a key indicator that this company may be a solid value investment, with everything else being equal.

Pay attention to accounts receivable. While a healthy level of accounts receivables is fine, a company that has an extremely high A/R level merits further and deeper analysis. It might be having a tough time collecting and you need to be very careful about how they log these. The company might only seem like it is worth a lot of money.

"Underappreciated Stocks"

Warren Buffett makes a big deal about underappreciated stocks. In fact, in many of his interviews, he talks about buying stocks that are under appreciated. Now, a lot of people would define "underappreciated stocks" as companies whose stock prices are a bargain compared to other companies in the Dow Jones Industrial Average.

This is a misconception. A stock is underappreciated in classical value investment terms not based on how it compares to other companies per se, but based on its potential future value. So in that context, a company that is selling for $50 a share now while other companies in its industry are selling for $40 a share, and its rate of appreciation is somewhat the same or slightly higher than the Dow Jones Industrial Average, can still be an underappreciated stock.

I know it sounds shocking, why? Compared to how it can grow in the future and what its potential fully realized value is in the long term future, its current stock price may be a bargain. Always keeps this in mind when doing value investing. Value investing doesn't necessarily mean penny pincher. It doesn't necessarily mean looking for discount stocks. It can very well mean that and you're basically buying at an immediate bargain compared to other stocks, but you should also factor in future value.

The stock may seem like it's well appreciated now, but given all the factors that I've outlined above, it might still be underappreciated and you would do well to lock in now. Remember, your strategy is to buy and hold. You're not looking to buy on a dip and unload on a recovery. You're just buying and holding for long term value.

The Risks of Value Investing

As solid as value investing may be, especially if you are setting money aside for your retirement, it also has its risks. First of all, let me point out the obvious. This investing strategy requires a very long time horizon. In fact, you shouldn't care about whether the stock spikes up or sinks down. All you care about is where the stock would be five, ten, fifteen, thirty years from now.

This is the time horizon value investors focus on. They look at the overall value of their portfolio and they focus on how much farther they would be ahead in dollars and cents when they cash out several years from now. This may seem good on paper, but it's not uncommon for a stock that you thought has a solid value to go through some rough years.

This happens quite a bit. When you buy the stock, it may be trading at $40 per share and then the next year, it goes through a rough patch and it sinks to $30. Then the year after that, it sinks another $10, to $20. At that point, you may be thinking to yourself that you made the wrong call but assuming that you did your homework properly, you really have nothing to worry about because you're in for the long game.

You're not holding the stock for just three years, you're holding the stock basically as an heirloom because you're going to cash out ten, twenty or thirty years from now. By that point, the stock price may have doubled or even tripled. Do you see how this works? Don't let the long time horizons get you down and scare you if the company goes through some reversals.

Another risk for value investing involves opportunity costs. If you have adopted a swing trading strategy, you may have been better off because you could have ridden several stocks up and down and realized faster gains. However, the whole opportunity cost argument is really only valuable if you're in a hurry. If on the other hand you are playing a long investment game with a long timeframe, then the opportunity costs are not really that big of an issue.

There's still an issue because you could have probably bought a better value stock, but all in all, the whole idea of wishing that you bought something else that you could have traded rapidly isn't an issue at all for a value investor.

Chapter 11: Playing the Stock Market through Mutual Funds

One of the best ways to minimize your risk playing the stock market is to essentially hire a professional to do it. That's exactly what you do when you buy a mutual fund. Every mutual fund has a manager or a set of managers. These people are professionals. These people know the financial industry. They've been around the block in terms of making the right calls, as far as stock purchases are concerned. They have a fairly good idea of when to buy and when to sell.

Still, despite their expertise, keep in mind that mutual funds have different rates of returns. Some mutual funds appreciate quite well. We're talking over 15% annual growth. Other mutual funds barely keep up with the annual rate of appreciation of the Dow Jones Industrial Average or major indexes. Others, unfortunately, underperform. Their rate of return is either negative or several points below the Dow Jones Industrial Average.

You have to use the Dow Jones Industrial Average as your basic metric because if you were to not do any research at all and just take your dollars and invest it in an index fund, that's the return you'll be getting. So this should be your benchmark as far as mutual funds are concerned. That is the rate of return that the fund manager is trying to beat. Pay attention to the following discussion so you can get a clear idea on how to pick a mutual fund.

Past Performance is not a Guarantee of Future Performance

The first thing that you need to keep in mind is that there is no shortage of mutual funds that seem to perform really well in the past. We're talking about 20% or even higher rates of appreciation. It's as if the party is going to go on forever. This mutual fund just keeps racking up amazing double digit growth year after year.

While it's easy to get excited about such funds, it's important to note that a larger a fund gets, the lower its rate of appreciation tends to become. This is not always the case, but that's the general trend, why? When you buy into a fairly small mutual fund or it's just starting out or it's just beginning its winning streak, since its capital base is fairly small, it can afford to go all in on certain stocks. And the rest of the market really won't notice.

Now, if the mutual fund is now worth several tens of billions of dollars in asset value and it's going to dump a huge chunk of those billions of dollars in one company, the market will sit up and pay attention. In other words, it's a victim of its success. It really can't operate under the radar, and chances are if it buys into a company, everybody else then buys in and there is a downward pressure that basically everything evens out as far as appreciation is concerned.

This is why when you look at a typical mutual fund, they've invested across a wide swath of companies within their target industries or in the companies that share the qualities that they're investing on. For example, growth stocks. Pay attention to this factor because it's easy to think that just because a company has grown like gang busters in the past that you are basically just locked into that rate of growth. It can very well turn out to be that the mutual fund is in for a correction the next few years. Maybe it was growing at a $20 annual rate. Maybe that can crash down to 2% or barely break even. It does happen.

The different types of Mutual Funds

There are many different types of mutual funds. Some focus on bonds, others focus on income assets. Meaning, these securities either pay a dividend or in the case of bonds, an interest. Other mutual funds focus on emerging markets like Brazil, Russia, and the Philippines. Pay attention to the different types of mutual funds out there. They have different investment strategies. They have different time horizons, as far as return on investment is concerned.

It's always a good idea to me sure that the overall investment philosophy of the mutual fund squares with yours because this increases the likelihood that you won't be disappointed, as far as your expectations are concerned.

Pay Attention to the Fees of a Mutual Fund

It's really important to pay attention to the management fees of a mutual fund. Understand that the company that runs the mutual fund is entitled to fees. They released this information publicly. This is what you buy into when you get into a mutual fund.

Read it very carefully because the fee might turn out to be too high and it might cut into the overall return that you get from the mutual fund, especially if the fund doesn't really perform all that well. Sure, it may still be worth higher than when you initially bought in but after all the fees have been taken out, it might just be basically limping by. That's not the kind of fund that you probably want to get into so pay attention to the fees.

Also pay attention to when you pay the fees. Is it a back loaded fund? Meaning, you get charged after you withdraw from the fund, or do you get charged before you get into the fund, which is a front loaded fund? This is a big factor as well. As much as possible, look for no load funds.

The problem with no load funds, however, is that they may have higher management fees so take a long hard look at the fee schedule and structure to see if the mutual fund company is being clever in hiding the fees, or if they play around with the timing of the load that you pay.

Figure out the Right Track Record Metrics

It's easy to get excited about a mutual fund that seems to be on a rampage. In its first year, it grew by 10%. The next year after that, it grew another 20%. It seems like a slam dunk, right? Well, pay attention to realistic metrics. While mutual funds have been shown to exhibit dramatic growth when analyzed in short timeframes, these exciting spikes actually flatten out if you look at a much longer time horizon.

The mutual fund might just be going through some hot years, but when you're looking at a 20 year timeframe for example, its performance might basically just be barely beating the Dow Jones Industrial Average for that same time period. Look at long term track record if you are buying long.

Now, if you're just going to be quickly going in and out of the mutual fund to lock in gains, then pay attention to the fees and how much they are, and when they kick in, as well as the performance record of the stock within a fairly short timeframe.

Chapter 12: Make Sure you have the Right Tools to Trade Profitably

If you are thinking of either buying into a mutual fund or trading individual stocks directly, you have to have the right tools. This is imperative. A lot of newbie investors think that one online brokerage is essentially the same all others. This is assuming too much, really.

You might be leaving a lot of money on the table by going with one online broker over another. You have to know what to look for. If you're just going to go by brand or by word of mouth, this might work against you. You might actually end up paying too much, seriously. You can pay too much in two ways.

First, you can pay too much in terms of just flat out higher fees. Different online brokers have different fees per trade. Some charge by volume, others charge by value, others charge a flat fee. Even among those that charge based off flat fee, their fees can differ.

The second way you pay is in terms of execution. You might be thinking, well if I order this stock to be bought and I bought it, where's the harm? Well, if you are using a platform that is fairly slow, you might not be getting the best price. It may be so slow, that you buy well after a pullback.

Meaning, if you're looking to buy into a stock, ideally you should buy in when the stock suffers a pullback or goes down in value. Now, the problem is if the trading platform is so slow, the pullback may have happened and now the stock is quickly recovering. And instead of for example buying a $30 stock at $25 pullback level, your platform gets you in at $27. You just lost $2. It might not seem like a big of a deal, but if you have a margin account and you're trading tens of thousands of shares, that can translate to a lot of money lost.

Do you see how this works? So make sure that you pay attention to the following factors when looking for the right tools to trade profitably. It doesn't really matter whether you're going to be doing a lot of trades every single day or you're basically just investing the stock market and adopting a position trading strategy where you just check in from time to time. This is also applicable if you are a value investor and you're just basically locking in now and then checking in once a year or twice a year.

Low Cost Trading Platform

The first thing that you need to look at is whether the platform is actually low cost. Compare the platform to other similar platforms. Look at their service package. What's the limit? How many shares can you buy and at what price before the commission or fee goes up? Make sure you compare apples to apples because some trading platforms use different fee schedules to try to trick you, but it turns out that on an aggregate basis, you may be paying more so do yourself a big favor. Make sure you're comparing apples to apples.

Fast Trading Platform

It's really important to make sure that your trades are executed as quickly as possible. Insist on a very fast platform because you may be out of a tremendous amount of money if you are investing in stock that is a high momentum or extremely volatile stock. It can be going up and down frequently with almost each and every trade and you want to lock in at the right price. This is much harder to pull off if you are using a trading platform that is fairly slow.

Fast Updating Charts

If you are a daily trader or a swing trader, you need charts. You need as much data in your charts so you can make the right call. You also need to make sure that you use charts that are updated frequently enough.

As much as possible, insist on real time updated charts. This enables you to make quick calls to seize pricing opportunities. For example, if a stock fell through the sport price and it looks like it's experiencing a nice pullback, you want to be able to see that pattern play out in real time on your chart so you can make strategic moves on when to capitalize on that change. This is very hard to do if your charts are unavailable or they update very slowly.

Solid Accountant

Taxes are a big issue if you're going to be trading stocks. US tax code treats stock trading income as regular income. Unless you're value investing and you just buy and sell stocks with more than one year intervals, you would have to pay regular income taxes on your trading income.

This is why it's really important to insist on solid accounting from your trading platform. The good news is by law, almost all trading platforms that offer their service in the United States have a solid accounting infrastructure. At the very least, your gains are being tracked, so you can report them to the IRS.

Make sure you use the right tools. If you want to increase the chances that you will trade profitably, you really cannot afford to use the wrong tools because at best, you'll be leaving a lot of money on the table and at worst, you'll be losing out.

Chapter 13: Day Trading Tactics

As I mentioned in the formal description of day trading, the whole point of this strategy is to trade within. We're not talking about a year and a half. We're not talking about two days. We're talking exactly within a day.

Now, at some level or other, the term day trading is actually a misnomer. It really is, because very successful day traders often don't need the whole day to make money. In many cases, they are tracking a stock and they get in and get out very quickly. In fact, in many cases, this action takes place in the span of an hour or a couple of hours. It definitely doesn't take the whole day to pull this off.

Still, when they've made a move, they've locked into a fairly substantial gain. Now, to a lot of people, a day trader's gain is nothing to write home about. I mean, after all, half a percentage point or a quarter of a percentage point seems a bit minuscule for many people.

You have to understand, however, that the main weapon of the day trader is volume. They trade big. They don't trade in like small lots like a hundred shares here and there. That's not going to move the ball. Instead, they trade in large chunks of cash. Hundreds of thousands of dollars is not uncommon.

Now, the interesting thing about all of this is that they're able to trade at such volumes and such dollar amount even if their actual capital is actually fairly modest. How are they able to do this?

Well, it's all about margin trading. Basically, they buy and sell stocks on credit. They take out a margin account from their brokerage account and in many cases, they don't even have to activate any account feature. The margin is already assumed. Accordingly, when you place an order using your brokerage platform, the margin is already indicated in your available funds.

In many cases, the brokerage platform will spell out how much of your actual cash you can trade with and how much extra margin you have available to you. It really all boils down to your discretion as to how much of your margin you would take advantage of. Make no mistake about it, thanks to the power of margin trading, day traders can turn what would otherwise be a fairly small microscopic gain into something substantial enough to live on a day to day basis.

There are many day traders who survive on their daily trading. In other words, that's how they make money. Whether we're talking about making a couple thousand dollars a day or tens of thousands of dollars a day, it's all about that daily return.

Now, I wish I could tell you that all day traders end up in the black every single day. Unfortunately, if I were to do that, I would be lying to you. Day trading is not for everybody. In fact, you really need a very strong gut and a lot of courage to day trade, because you have to liquidate your position, regardless of whether you're up or down at the end of the day. There are no exceptions.

Otherwise, you're not day trading. Otherwise, you're using a different strategy. Maybe you're doing swing trading or position trading, but you're definitely not doing day trading. Day trading is all about quick in and out positions, whether you're riding the stock up, or you're riding it down by selling short.

What follows are some common day trading tactics that you can experiment with to increase the amount of gains you experience every single day. Now, just like with anything else in life, the more you try something, the better you get at it. What's important here is not to focus on earning the big bucks early on. Instead, focus on learning the day trading strategy so you can get your bearings. The moment you have your sea legs is the moment you will be able to fully map out the extent of the opportunities in front of you.

Make no mistake about it, day trading is not investing. A lot of people have this misconception. They think that day traders are stock investors. No, they're not. A day trader really doesn't care about the long-term potential of a company. All the day trader looks at are technical indicators.

What are the technical indicators that a day trader zeroes in on? First, is volume. How much volume is there in a stock on the buying side and on the selling side? Just by comparing the relative interest that traders have to buy or sell a stock, you can get a rough idea as to whether the stock is poised for a breakout because there is a lot of pent-up demand or it's basically ripe for a crash.

While classical day traders were able to do this using spreadsheets and manual analysis, there are sophisticated software that you can buy that will spell out this information for you and present it in an easy to understand graphical form. One common way of depicting information is called the "candlestick" graphic. The candlestick would show the bottom price of a stock and the top price of a stock within the day. It would also indicate the volume involved.

By paying attention to your software, you can make educated guesses to where to buy in and when to sell the stock. It's important to make sure that you have the right tools because the tactics that I'm going to lay out below require very fast information. You need to have very quick information to execute your trade as soon as possible, because with day trading, if you wait one minute, you may have vaporized your profit for the day. That's how sensitive day trading can be.

Now, some stocks are more sensitive than others, but by and large, you need a platform that can execute trades very quickly. You also need investment tools that can get breaking real time information so you can make truly informed decisions. Here are just some day trading tactics you can experiment with.

Scalping

When you scalp, you sell a stock after it makes a minimal profit increase. It doesn't really matter how much the profit is. Maybe it's a couple of cents or maybe it's a quarter. You're not looking for the stock to gain a dollar or something substantive like that. What you're really looking for is some positive increase in the stock's value.

Now, again, for this to work out, you have to play with volume. If you only had a thousand dollars and you're doing scalping, it would probably take you forever to turn that thousand dollars into two thousand dollars because the increases that you're locking into are often below 1%. However, if you're using your margin funds, you can multiply the amount of appreciation your capital is capable of achieving. This scalping is definitely a margin play.

Now, it all depends on how much of a percentage gain you're looking for. Some day traders are perfectly happy with a 1% gain. Others insist on 2% and more. What should inform your answer really boils down to how active the stock is. If you're trading a stock that is extremely volatile and can pop up and down fairly quickly, you have a lot more room to play as long as there are a lot of buyers and there is a lot of turnover in the stock. You can set up your day trades in such a way that if the stock experiences a nice run up for its inter-day trading range, you can lock in at or near the high point to walk away with a decent chunk of cash.

How much money can you make off scalping? Well, it depends on how much capital and margin you are working with. If you're dealing with a capital base that is in the tens of thousands of dollars, or hundreds of thousands of dollars, it's not uncommon for you to achieve a daily gain of a couple to a few thousand dollars per day.

As exciting as all these may sound, keep in mind that you're going to be paying taxes on those trading gains. According to the IRS, trading gains are regular income. This is why it's really important to make sure that your trading software has a solid reporting system so you can see exactly how much profit you made and how much of the profit will go to taxes. It's important to keep setting aside tax payments so you don't get in trouble when tax time rolls around.

Fading

Let's just get one thing out of the way. Fading is a very lucrative, yet extremely risky day trading tactic. The great thing about buying long regardless of how short your timeframe may be is that a stock, technically speaking, can go up infinitely. In other words, the upside can be as high as you can imagine.

Maybe you're dealing us with a stock that is $10 right now per share. Its upside potential is really limitless. Maybe the company is being run by a visionary like Steve Jobs. Then, in that case, it's not outside the realm of possibility for the stock to double, triple, or even quadruple in price. The upside potential is basically inexhaustible.

Now, compare this with the other direction. The other direction, of course, is to play the stock short. In other words, you're going to borrow the stock from your brokerage and the sell it at a high price and then buy it back once it hits a bottom. In that $10 stock example, the upside potential for you is essentially $10. That's the amount of money the stock can drop.

Now, compare these two scenarios. Which would you rather work with, an almost unlimited upside potential or a $10 future potential gain? I need you to think in those terms because a lot of beginning investors think that short selling is some sort of magic strategy. They think that's short selling can make them millionaires. Well, not quite.

If the stock you are dealing with is so inexpensive and the existing total amount of shares at play is not that substantial, your gains might be very modest. They are potential gains may be very modest. In that particular situation, the risks that you take might just completely outweigh whatever you stand to gain. Always consider this when thinking of doing short sales.

Fading is short selling for day traders. They sell short when the stock, as they think, hit a high point for the day. Once the stock dips again, they then put in a limit order to buy back the stock. This means that they vacated their short position. That they end up making money on the difference between the high point and the price point on which they bought or "covered" the stock.

Make no mistake about it, selling stocks short can be quite lucrative. You are essentially betting that the stock will dip. The good news is that there is no stock that is immune to this. Even Apple Computers' stock is not immune to this. There are always bound to be pullbacks.

Accordingly, you are bound to see a stock drop in price. The problem is timing. This is really the art of short selling. It's when you sell the stock short and when you cover it, it all boils down to the proper timing.

Time it right and you can earn a profit. Time it wrong and you might get a margin call and end up losing quite a bit of cash

Pivot

A pivot trade is a bit of a longer strategy for day traders. For a lot of day traders, scalping is the norm. Basically, they take a stock and wait for it to appreciate even for a very small amount or a tiny fraction of a percent, and then they exit. Pretty straightforward. Very clean.

A pivot, on the other hand, requires a much larger appreciation. What they would do is they would try to buy at the low point of the day and then sell the stock at its highest point in the day. Now, what's scary about day trading is that the longer you wait, the higher the likelihood that you probably would lose money. That's just the reality of day trading.

However, the good news is this high-risk situation also creates a high reward possibility. While it's true that you are waiting for a much longer period after you bought what you thought was the low point of the day so you can unload at the high point. This wait can be rewarded by much greater gain because you timed your sales correctly.

Of course, the way to do this is to put a stop limit sell order good for the particular price point that you think would constitute the stock's high point for the day. You need the discipline to pull this off. Otherwise, you're not doing day trading. Otherwise, you're basically doing swing trading or position trading.

The discipline here is even if the stock doesn't hit your high point projection where you planned to exit, you still need to liquidate your position. The reason why you're doing this is it frees you up to try a pivot play again the next day. In other words, you're not going to be stuck with opportunity costs where you're just waiting for the stock to move one way or the other, while it basically trades sideways.

You end up paying some cash in terms of a moderate loss for you to avoid opportunity costs. So regardless of whether you have hit a high spot, or you barely made money, or you even lost a little bit of money, you need to exit within the day.

Momentum Tactic

A momentum play is when there is a tremendous amount of velocity in a stock. This happens quite a bit with biotechnology stocks. For example, if a stock has an FDA filing and the US Food and Drug Administration approved the biotechnology company's filing, this can explode the value of the stock.

It's not uncommon for biotechnology stocks to double or even triple in price the same day. Indeed, 50% rises in value are quite expected, especially if the biotechnology stock is all but a penny stock prior to the big announcement. You have to set up your software to be on the lookout for stocks that are seeing massive gains in price, as well as volume.

Many stock trading platforms have this search technology. You should use them, either as a direct feature or as a premium add-on. Whatever the case may be, you need to use them so you can get on top of stocks that are on the go. The key here is to lock in at a stock while it's still fairly low and then graduate your gains.

For example, based on your analysis of the momentum of the stock, you might be thinking that it will go up 50% in price so to protect yourself, you can set up your account to liquidate your position at 50% of your position if the stock appreciates by a certain percentage point. You then still are left in the stock for the other 50% of your investment, and you then set up another schedule of that where you exit half of that if the stock continues to go up.

This way, you lock in on a nice appreciation and if the stock does peter out in its upwards trajectory, you have still locked in on some gains. These are quite exciting. But again, you're not investing. You're not paying attention to the news as much as you're paying attention to the technical impact of the news on the company's stock.

You have to keep it technical. Don't get taken in by the implications of the news otherwise, you might end up staying too long in the stock and it might not go all that well for you.

Keep in mind that momentum trading also works in reverse. You can ride up a stock that is on fire. As it goes up in value very quickly, you can ride it up. Now, once you notice that the volume of sellers are picking up, you can also ride it down. This is when you start selling the stock short.

Accordingly, you make money from the stock in two ways. You make money when it is appreciating, and you make money when it is depreciating value. Pretty straightforward. Again, it takes a lot more guts to sell a stock short because if a stock is volatile, it may take only one huge purchase for the stock price to spike back up, and you might get hit with a nasty margin call because all your short gains basically evaporated.

Chapter 14: Position Trading Tactics

If you are using position trading strategy, the tactics that you can use are going to be quite different from the tactics used by a day trader or a value trader. There's a lot of fluidity with position trading, but since you're going to be camping out on the stock for quite a while, you have a lot more leeway than day trading.

Even if there were some adverse movements in the stock you're invested in for several days, you still can gain some measure of comfort from the fact that you're in for a longer duration. You do have the luxury, at some level or other, of weathering out the storm.

With that said, there are some key tactics that you need to be aware of so you can maximize your gains. A key tactic for position trading is to buy on the dips. Since you know that you're going to be leaving the stock only after it has hit your target price, what happens when the stock actually sinks in value? For example, you take out a position at $10 per share. The stock proceeds to trade and it promptly sinks to $5 a share. This is actually an opportunity. You can do dollar cost averaging. What this means is when you buy the same amount of stocks that you did at $10 at the new entry price of $5, your effective entry value is $7.50.

Accordingly, when the stock reaches that point and proceeds northwards, you are in the black. Do you see how this works? So don't get scared when a stock basically dips in price. In fact, it could be an opportunity because if you buy the same amount as before, you lower the price point over which you make a profit.

Now, if you were to buy way more at the lower price than when you bought in originally, you decrease the break-even point quite a bit. In fact, if you buy enough, you can, for all practical purposes, reduce that breakeven point to the new low price of the stock.

This is a very important technique for position traders because when you're taking out a fairly long range of position on a stock, it's anybody's guess where that's stock would go. It would be nice if the shares keep going up in value, but we know that's not true. There will be dips and depending on the stock that you're following, the dips can be very harsh. We're talking about a 50% pullback. That's not all that uncommon.

Always remember dollar cost averaging because this can reduce your breakeven point and if you stick to your original sell price, you might actually make a lot more money than previously. With that said, for dollar cost averaging to work, you have to have some cash stored away in your account. This is cash that you're not using for trading.

One way to get this cash is to, of course, tap into your margin account. Still, it's important to keep in mind that if you're going to access that margin cash, make sure that you are confident that the dip that the stock recently experienced is the bottom because if it keeps crashing, then you might be in serious trouble because of a margin call. Take note of the following tactics when doing position trading.

Be Aware of the News Cycle

Every stock basically has its own news cycle. For example, all stocks have earnings cycles. Every single year, public companies are required by the Securities and Exchange Commission to release financial documents for their performance for the previous quarter. These are quarterly results required by the US SEC. Be aware of these dates so you can gauge market sentiment as these dates approach.

Why is this important? Well, if the consensus for a stock is that they would have earnings of say, 10 cents a share, and the actual performance of the stock is exactly 10 cents. That may not do much for the company's stock. And in fact, if the stock is heavily traded, it might even drag down the price of the stock.

However, if the stock actually beats expectations, this can lead to a really nice bump up in the stock's price. Now, always keep this in mind because the news cycles may stack up in such a way that you would be able to leave your position sooner rather than later. If there's a high enough appreciation and you're basically saying that you only want a 25% gain for the year, this might be it.

By the same token, if the stock performs horribly and disappoints people and the stock tanks, being aware of the news cycle can also be a good thing. You can then do some dollar cost averaging when the stock tanks and wait for the next earnings report to try to gauge when you would like to exit.

Research specific Companies or Industries

Position trading involves more research than day trading. With day trading, you're just paying attention to the technical information involved. You're just looking for volume, as well as the number of buyers, and the number of sellers, as well as the block sizes. With position trading, you're taking such a long position that it makes sense for you to research the specific company and its prospects within a larger block of time.

It's also important to brown this information in terms of what's going on and its broader industry. Using these two data points, you should have a fairly rough idea of how the company's stock might perform based on its news cycle.

Find potential Breakout Stars

If you do a sufficient amount of research about specific companies and industries, a few companies might stand out. These companies are on the verge of releasing a new product or they may be on the verge of profitability. Whatever the case may be, they're going to be experiencing positive developments that can have a very significant impact on their stock price.

It's important to look at who the potential breakout stars are and then cross reference their previous weeks' trading patterns. You have to understand that you're not the only investor looking for a great deal. There are many professional investors out there. There are many highly paid financial analysts looking for the same information as you.

When you look at the previous weeks' trading patterns for potential breakout stars, you might be able to tell if some experts or even mutual funds are already buying into the company. How do you know? Well, pay attention to one factor: volume. The volume of trades for a stock pretty much reveals its upside potential.

If you notice that a lot of institutional investors are buying into a stock and yet a stock price doesn't really move all that much, this may indicate that you're looking at a potential breakout star. Now, this is not a slam dunk. There are companies that regardless of how much buying action takes place, they never go anywhere because their industry is not that sexy, seriously.

For example, utilities are not very sexy. However, tech stocks like internet stocks are very sexy, regardless of whether the company's making a profit or not. So always factor that in. Volume levels speak very loudly regarding whether a stock is a potential breakout star or not.

Chapter 15: Value Trading Tactics

If you're a value stock investor, your tactics are going to be very different from those used by a position trader, a day trader, or a swing trader. Your goal is to thoroughly invest in a company. Unlike a day trader who just looks at technical information like volume and trajectory, a value trader looks at the actual guts of the company. You look at the factors influencing the value of a company now and its current potential.

You also pay attention to its long-term potential. As I've mentioned previously, a value trader isn't necessarily scared off by high stock prices. For example, if you come across a company that is currently valued at $100 per share, a lot of people might think that given its current earnings, this is too high a price to pay to get into that company.

However, if you look at its potential future value, as well as its trajectory within its industry, $100 might well prove to be quite a bargain. Do you see how this works? Value traders aren't fazed high stock prices or scared off by low stock prices. Instead, they don't really care about the conventional wisdom regarding the company. They just look at whether its current value or its projected future value makes it a good acquisition.

Also, when you're doing value trading, you are investing for the long haul. This is why when the price of that stock drops, you view this as good news. You really do. Why? You're buying it a bigger bargain. You already think it's a bargain now, that's why you're buying in, but when the stock experiences a setback and its price drops down, this is nothing short of good news for you.

You keep buying in regardless of where the price is until you have put together enough shares for your portfolio. Given these parameters, the tactics used by value orders are quite different from those of other types of traders using different strategies. Please note the following.

Shortcut Technique

This is one shortcut technique value traders can benefit from. If you don't have the time effort or energy to do extensive, as well as intensive research on the stocks you're thinking of adding to your value investment portfolio, simply reverse engineer the homework of professionals.

How do you do this? Look at very successful mutual funds that have appreciated quite a bit over a long period of time. We're talking about ten years of solid performance. Look at their performance and then look at their reported holdings. The SEC requires mutual funds to report the names of the companies that they have taken large positions in.

By accessing this list and buying accordingly, you save yourself a tremendous amount of time effort and money because you don't have to pay anybody for this research. The expert mutual fund manager is forced to basically spill the beans as to which companies they bought into for their portfolio. Now, this can be a little bit tricky because it can very well turn out that a mutual fund would buy a lot of stocks in a company, and then report it, and it turns out that they exited the company right after reporting time.

If you were to take buy into that company, you might be buying into a stock which has a value that is basically tapped out. Meaning, its total appreciation has already been captured by other investors and it is either going to track sideways or it might even dip down. This is a key risk with reverse engineering.

So pay attention to timing. Also, you might want to diversify your stock purchases among different mutual funds holdings. This way you're leveraging the expertise of not just one expert, but many.

Pay close Attention to Long-Range Industry Trends

Look for industries that are very solid and are poised to grow. It's important to make sure that you lock in on growth. An industry must be growing. It can't be mature and contracting. That's not going to do you much good. So buy industry reports to see which parts of the American economy are going and are showing positive trends. These are the industries that you are then going to focus on to find rising companies that are already public.

Focus on existing public companies that are top players or are fast-rising players in growing industries

Now, the funny thing about industry growth is it's too easy to get in over your head. It's too easy to get so excited about red-hot growth. The problem with red-hot growth is in most cases, it's not sustainable.

For example, if there is a new industry like 3D printing or digital data streaming. In the beginning, it's going to show red-hot growth but after a while, it's going to stabilize and then consolidate. In other words, the initial spike up might actually flat line, or it may even fall off a cliff.

I need you to understand this because it's too easy to get all excited about industry trends because things are coming up roses currently. You have to look past near-term projections and look for the long range projection. Is this industry going to be around five to ten years from now? How prone is it to disruption? Is there a likelihood that the industry would collapse into another industry?

By asking these strategic questions, you position yourself to identify industries that are worth following. Once you've done that, then you look at their existing top players or fast rising players.

Look at their balance sheets, look at their total debt load, and other fundamental qualities. If you noticed that a company is fairly undervalued, yet have strong fundamentals, that company might be a good value play.

Key advice for Value Trading

My key advice for value trading is that you have to assign yourself more conservative cash to this. What I mean by conservative cash is that this is capital that you expect to grow over the long haul. This is not your risk capital that you intentionally invest in highly risky stocks so you can lock in on amazing rewards. Instead, this is the capital that you are thinking of retiring on. This is long range capital.

Conclusion

Making money on stocks doesn't have to be a big mystery. It doesn't have to be a gamble. By being clear on what your needs, are as well as the trading strategies available to you, you can put together a plan of action that can help you mix successful trades, not just once in a while, but basically every single time.

It all boils down to learning curve. You have to stick to the learning curve. You have to basically learn what you need to learn and take the necessary risks until you get the hang of it. Put in another way, if it was very easy then everybody would be a billionaire. Obviously, that's not the case. You have to stick to it and you need to put in the time to learn what you need to learn to develop enough expertise to at least trade profitably consistently.

Profitable trading, of course, means more than break even. Whether it's a dollar or hundreds of thousands of dollars, it's up to you. I wish you nothing but the greatest abundance and success in your trading.

Find this Book Valuable? Why not leave an Honest Review on Amazon!

I believe this book shared you all the necessary information you needed to understand stock market investing better and apply it to your investing strategies in order to become an intelligent investor and making money in stocks.

The next step is to implement what you have learnt.

Finally, if you enjoyed this book and received value out of it then I'd like to ask you for a favor. Would you be kind enough to leave a review for this book on Amazon? It'd be greatly appreciated!

Leaving review only takes a few seconds and it will enable me to continue to produce high quality, enriching content to serve people like you.

As we learnt the powerful stock market investing strategies, I want to reach as many people as I can with this book in order to share the benefits of these strategies to maximum people. The higher the number of reviews, the more people I can reach!

The more positive reviews the book gets, the more others will be able to find the book, purchase it and experience the benefits of stock investing.

Printed in Great Britain
by Amazon